THE COMPLETE GUIDE TO YOUR FIRST HORSE FOR YOUNG RIDERS

ALL ABOUT HORSE HISTORY, HEALTH, CARE, ANATOMY, AND PHYSIOLOGY TO BECOME A BETTER HORSEMAN AND HAVE A DEEPER BOND WITH YOUR PARTNER

ELISA KING

© **Copyright 2023 - All rights reserved.**

The content contained within this book may not be reproduced, duplicated or transmitted without direct written permission from the author or the publisher.

Under no circumstances will any blame or legal responsibility be held against the publisher, or author, for any damages, reparation, or monetary loss due to the information contained within this book, either directly or indirectly. You are responsible for your own choices, actions, and results.

Legal Notice:

This book is copyright protected. It is only for personal use. You cannot amend, distribute, sell, use, quote or paraphrase any part, or the content within this book, without the consent of the author or publisher.

Disclaimer Notice:

Please note the information contained within this document is for educational and entertainment purposes only. All effort has been executed to present accurate, up to date, reliable, complete information. No warranties of any kind are declared or implied. Readers acknowledge that the author is not engaged in the rendering of legal, financial, medical or professional advice. The content within this book has been derived from various sources. Please consult a licensed professional before attempting any techniques outlined in this book.

By reading this document, the reader agrees that under no circumstances is the author responsible for any losses, direct or indirect, that are incurred as a result of the use of the information contained within this document, including, but not limited to, errors, omissions, or inaccuracies.

CONTENTS

Introduction   9

1. HUMANS AND HORSES – A HISTORY   15
   The Origins of Today's Horses   16
   Life With Man— The Early Years   17

2. ALL ABOUT THE HORSE   21
   A Foal is Born   22
   What About Ponies?   25
   Story: A Big-Hearted Horse   28

3. HOW HORSES ARE BUILT   29
   Major Parts of the Horse   30
   Hidden Parts   32

4. A HORSE OF A DIFFERENT COLOR   43
   But No Green Ones?   44
   All Those White Markings!   50
   Story: A Rescue Turned Champion   59

5. FEEDING YOUR HORSE   61
   Water   62
   Food   63
   How Much Food?   70

6. BARN MANAGEMENT 101   73
   A Paddock and Run-In   74
   Box Stalls   76
   Types of Fencing   79
   Story: The Mystery of a Kidnapped Racing Star   84

7. DAILY HORSE CARE 89
   Safety First 90
   Grooming 93
   Story: Not as Famous as Dad 104

8. THE MIND OF THE HORSE 107
   How to Read a Horse 108
   Flight or Fight 114
   Overall Appearance 116
   Story: The Most Famous Horse in the
   Movies 117

9. INJURIES AND ILLNESS 119
   Injuries - Bruises, Nicks, Cuts, Scrapes,
   and Worse 120
   Common Health Issues 124
   Story: Old Billy and Friends 133

10. GET READY TO RIDE! 135
    Preparing for a Ride 136
    Your Tack 138
    Caring for Your Tack 148
    Tacking Up Your Horse 150
    What Will You Wear? 153

11. RIDING BASICS 155
    Mounting and Dismounting 156
    How to Sit on a Horse 159
    Story: Two Boys and a Pony 164

12. HORSE SPORTS AND ACTIVITIES 167
    Racing 168
    Rodeos 170
    Team Sports 172
    Eventing 172
    Horse Shows 174
    And So Much More 175
    Clubs and Groups 177

Conclusion	183
Appendix I	185
Appendix II	187
Glossary	191
About the Author	195
References	197

Allergy Warning: Allergies to horse dander and hay can be serious. Please consult a medical professional if you think you are allergic or show any symptoms before getting involved with horses.

INTRODUCTION

> *A horse doesn't care how much you know until he knows how much you care.*
>
> — PAT PARELLI

Calling all horse lovers! Whether you own your own horse, ride one at the local farm, or have visions of having your own pony in the garage, there is always so much to know. Horses are beautiful creatures, and humans have been drawn to them for thousands of years. Back in the day, most families had a horse or two for driving the carriage to town, or helping with the farm work, or both. In old villages, you might see a lot of garages that look like barns because they once were! Horses were part tractor and part family car. A visit to relatives might have taken days instead of a few hours, but your trusty horse would get you there—eventually. Horses were our year-round friends and workmates. They came with their own four-wheel drive, and cart wheels could be switched to sleigh runners for winter travel. Horses have powered ferries and forges using pulleys and treadmills. They have even been our warrior partners, bringing soldiers into battle and pulling cannons.

Today, horses are primarily a luxury item used for a variety of equestrian sports and activities. For those of us who love them, they are more like a necessity. Yes, some people still farm with horses and horses are used for logging—pulling those big trees out of the woods and collecting sap in spring to make syrup. There is still one small town near me with a long wagon pulled by two big, gray draft horses that works as the village's trash truck!

The walls of your room may or may not be covered in horse posters (mine weren't), and the shelves may or may not be home to horse books and figurines (definitely yes to the books), but does that make you a horse person? Maybe yes, maybe no. How much do you know about horses and their care, what they are thinking and feeling, and how to tell if they are sick? What about different sports, breeds, and colors? If you ride, do you ever wonder how the horse spends the rest of the day? Do you know what it eats, whether it sleeps, and if it has any horse friends? You don't need to be a rider to be a good horseman, but being a rider doesn't automatically make you a horseman. The best riders are both. They know how to care for their horse and what its basic needs are. They know basic vocabulary specific to horses. Even some of the best equine veterinarians and farriers don't ride, but they do know all about horses. Above all, one thing all true horse lovers have in common is that they always want to learn more about them.

If you are lucky, there might be a horse club or camp at a stable nearby that you can join to learn more. Perhaps there is a 4-H or Pony Club. Even some YMCAs offer horse-focused camps and programs. If you are really lucky, maybe there is a horse in your life already; if not your own then maybe a parent or sibling has one. Does the neighbor down the road have horses? Ask them if you can come help out around the barn in exchange for learning about horse and stable management. Helping out means everything from brushing and grooming to picking up manure to scrubbing out water troughs. Be ready to work and be eager to do whatever is needed. Nothing beats "hooves on" experience!

Owning your own horse is many a horse lover's dream. It definitely is, and it's also hard work. Horses are strong and sturdy, yet impossibly fragile. They need good food, clean water, and a nice place to rest. They will need to see a doctor, or veterinarian, at least for routine care, and also a dentist to make sure those big teeth are in good working order for grinding hay, or eating carrots. Getting to know your vet and farrier will help you develop a good relationship with them as you both care for your horse. If you don't have your own, ask those horse-owning neighbors if you can come watch the next time the vet or farrier comes to their house.

While owning your own horse can seem like a dream, it is also a huge responsibility. They need attention twice a day, every day—even on weekends and holidays. And it's not just the horse care. It's your job to keep them safe. Your fences need to be checked regularly and well-maintained, and your barn or shelter should be kept in good repair at all times. Rotten boards or posts, and loose nails and wires all pose significant hazards to your equine buddy.

Are you wondering if it's all worth it by now, or are you thinking it looks easy? Well, it isn't easy, but can be fun and incredibly rewarding. Imagine your friend cantering across a meadow, mane and tail flying. Can you think of anything more beautiful? Let's get a few steps closer to that reality; let's start learning all about horses!

Note: because geldings (castrated males) are the most common to be owned as family pets or personal riding horses, we will refer to the horse as "he," "they," or "it" throughout this book, unless we are specifically referring to a stallion (an intact breeding male), a mare (adult female), a colt, or filly (a mare or stallion less than three years old).

1

HUMANS AND HORSES – A HISTORY

> *How blessed are we that nature saw fit to honor our presence on earth with the gift of the horse!*
>
> — C. FAIRCHILD

Horses have been on the planet far longer than humans have. When they first appeared, they came in a variety of colors, shapes, markings, and sizes. Some were as small as a fox, and some were comparable to small horses of today. Most had three toes instead of one hoof; vestiges of these two toes can still be found on modern horses today. For about 55 million years, these animals lived peacefully side by side, mostly browsing on trees and shrubs for food, while a few nibbled grasses when they could. These ancestors shared the suffix of "hippus" or "ippus" to their latin names.

THE ORIGINS OF TODAY'S HORSES

Beginning around 20 million years ago, as the earth changed and grasslands began to expand, these creatures grew and evolved into the animal we know today as Equus. During the Miocene era, a period from approximately 11–14 million years ago, the single-hoofed grazing animal *Dinohippus* or *Pilohippus* remained after their three-toed, shrub-browsing relatives gradually died off. *Dinohippus* had many similarities to Equus besides diet and hoof structure. From what scientists have learned, they had the same skeletal structure that horses have now. It's this structure that makes it possible for them to carry us without breaking in half.

Looking somewhat like a cross between a small horse, a donkey, and a zebra, early Equus was the precursor to the whole Equidae family that includes: horses, ponies, zebras, wild asses, and donkeys. Equus caballus as a distinct species only includes animals that look like today's horses, like *Przewalski's horse*, a modern-day true wild horse, and all the breeds of domestic horses and ponies.

LIFE WITH MAN— THE EARLY YEARS

There was a very, very long time before man, in some form, encountered the horse. Yet, it did not take long for those early humans to develop a deep relationship with them. Horses fed and clothed us, helped us hunt, gave us milk, and allowed us to more easily migrate with the seasons. It was 20 million years ago that horses began to evolve; it was only 2.5 million years ago when the creatures that would become known as "man" began to roam the earth. Many groups of human-like species came, evolved, began the journey to walking upright, then died out. The species we recognize as man only arrived about 750,000 years ago. Still, the first evidence of humans and horses being in contact came during that earlier period of the late ice age, or Pleistocene era.

Predator and Prey

It seems at that time, Neanderthal man ate horse meat and used horse hide and bone from animals they scavenged, not hunted. Fossil remains found in France show that prehistoric man began hunting horses for food and clothing about 37,000 years ago. Horses were rounded up in small areas at the base of a cliff. The area was contained by rocks and stones to create a makeshift corral. Archeologists believe these events happened twice a year, in spring and fall, when herds of horses were migrating to better grazing lands.

In North America, hunting horses seems to have begun around 13,000 years ago. Grasslands to the north that emerged after the ice retreated provided ample grazing for a variety of large animals, including horses, buffalo, ancient breeds of mountain goats and sheep, and members of the family that includes deer, moose, and elk.

A Change in the Game

Although scientists don't all agree on the exact timing, somewhere between four and six thousand years ago, horses first became domesticated in eastern Europe, in an area known as the Eurasian Steppe—the world's largest temperate grassland. The Steppe covers a long area from Hungary to China that extends almost 20% of the way around the globe. They were still used for meat, and their hides and bones for clothing, shelter, and tools, but they were also bred for their milk and to increase herd size and quality. These horses were also bred to the wild horses that still remained.

Before climbing on the backs of horses, humans did ride other animals. Oxen and onagers (distant relatives to Equus caballus—a sort of zebra-horse-antelope creature) were the first to carry us. Both were more suited to the job, being easier to domesticate and train than horses. Oxen in particular were strong enough to work and pull as well as carry people long distances. But they were not fast. Onagers were smaller, but likely much faster, with a quiet demeanor making them easy to train. We know horses to be fight or flight animals, their temperaments making them not easily trainable. Their relatively small size in the beginning also made them less useful for long trips and carrying heavy loads. Research indicates that we finally began riding horses about 5,000 years ago. The rest, as they say, is history!

Did You Know?

The last member of the Equus family that was native to North America was Equus scotti. Measuring about four and a half feet tall at the shoulder and seven feet long from nose to tail, Equus scotti was a closer relative to today's zebras than horses.

Found all over the continent, Equus scotti had a single hoof instead of three toes, lived in small herds, and was a grazer rather than a browser. Fossils indicate that they appeared about 2 million years ago, and went extinct about 10,000 years ago.

Przewalski's horse is distinct from Equus caballus in a few important ways, one being that they have an extra pair of chromosomes in their genes (66 vs 64). This means they have the ability to mate with domestic horses and any other member of the Equus caballus family, such as donkeys or zebras. All the offspring will look like Przewalski's: A heavily built, small, stocky horse with a thick neck and shortish legs. They range in height from 13–15 hands and weigh 550 to 800 pounds. They can tolerate temperature ranges from 104 to -50 degrees fahrenheit.

The coat is like a dun without a mask, including the dorsal strip and hints of zebra stripes on the upper leg and withers. They lack a forelock, and their upright mane is darker down the center than along the sides.

Originally found around the Gobi desert near the Mongolian Steppes, their diet consists of grasses and browsing from shrubs. At one time extinct in the wild, they have been reintroduced to areas near Kazakhstan, Mongolia, and China.

They are the only true wild horses remaining; any other horses called "wild" are actually feral—domesticated animals that have returned to a life in the wild.

2

ALL ABOUT THE HORSE

> *I am still under the impression that there is nothing alive quite so beautiful as a horse.*
>
> — JOHN GALSWORTHY

It's fun to know a bit more about the ancient history of horses, and how and when we started to interact with them. It's even more fun to learn about the horses we know and love today! From a foal's first days to old horses still at work, we'll look at how horses grow, what their days might be like, and all about different types and breeds.

A FOAL IS BORN

In wild herds, there is one mature stallion, several younger stallions, and a number of mares. There are also young horses ranging from newborn to two years old or older—the foals from previous years. The dominant mare helps the herd find good grazing and water, while the stallion protects them from intruding stallions. It is most often the mares that keep watch for predators and alert the others, although any one of the group may set off an alarm. Wild horses breed in early spring, and that is when breeders—those who raise horses—of domestic horses also start the cycle. Breeding early in the year means that foals are born early the following spring, giving them the best chance to grow and develop while the weather is nice and there is lots of food available.

A mare, the word for both a mother and any female horse over three years old, carries her baby for 11 months—that's almost a full year! After being bred to the stallion, who is called a sire once his first offspring are born, the mare has nothing more to do with him; it's just her and her foal from now on. Many of the abilities we see in horses today come from those times thousands of years ago, when horses were truly wild and were also a good source of food for predators. It's why still today foals can stand up, nurse from their mothers, and walk within an hour or so of being born. Only a few hours later, they can run. If a predator comes along, that newborn foal will need to run away with its mother and the herd.

This two-day-old colt shows he's ready to run with the herd.

Foal, Filly, or Colt?

A young horse, whether male or female, is called a foal. When it reaches between four and six months old, it is still a foal, but is called a weanling. This means the foal no longer relies on its mother's milk to survive, and is going through a process called weaning—transitioning from an all-milk diet to solid food.

At one year, young horses are known as yearlings until their third birthday. The words foal, weanling, and yearling apply to both male and female young; male foals are called colts and females are fillies. Once they reach age three, they are known as stallions and mares. Most of the male horses you know are called geldings, since they have been castrated, or neutered, and cannot produce offspring.

Growing Up

Within a foal's first six months, they will develop their baby deciduous or "milk" teeth, and can begin to eat grass and other solid foods like grains. By the end of their first year, they will grow to about 2/3 of their adult size. An average-sized horse weighs only about 100 pounds at birth, a yearling will more than triple their weight in the first year, and by age two will be close to their mature weight of almost 1,000 pounds. But they aren't fully grown on the outside until they are four years old, and some of their bones will not have completed growing until they are six!

As the foal ages, it's a good idea to keep an eye on its growth, both in height and weight. A horse's height is measured in *hands*. Each hand is four inches. Starting at the ground by the front hoof, and being slow and careful so as not to startle the horse, use a tape measure or specially made height stick to find out the total number of inches at the top of the *withers*, or the high bump above the shoulder, just about where their mane ends. Then divide that number by four. If your foal measures 48 inches, then they are 12 hands tall. An average adult horse is 15.3 hands; that measurement can vary widely from breed to breed and even from one horse to another of the same breed.

To get an idea of how much your horse weighs, use a soft, specially designed weight tape. Wrap it around the body of the horse just behind the withers and in back of the elbow. This area is the horse's *heartgirth*—the circumference of the horse that goes around the rib cage where the heart is, and follows the line where the girth, or belt, of the saddle goes. Now just read the number! This method will not give a perfectly accurate weight, but it will give you a baseline so you can watch for weight gain or loss.

WHAT ABOUT PONIES?

While ponies and horses are the same species of animal and belong to the same family, Equus caballus (see chapter one), there are some notable differences. Size is the most obvious, but not necessarily the most reliable. There are some horse breeds that can be small, less than 14.2 hands, which is considered the maximum height for ponies, or a little over four and a half ft tall at the withers. Morgans, Arabians, Paso Finos, Icelandic horses, and Quarter horses are just a few examples. Some pony breeds can be over that height, such as Welsh ponies or Connemaras. The term "true ponies" is used to differentiate small animals of a horse breed versus Shetland, Welsh, Pony of the Americas, Fell, Exmoor, and Dartmoor pony breeds, among others.

Some important characteristics that set ponies apart include their rate of growth and maturity, their temperament, and their robust constitution. Ponies grow and mature much more quickly than horses. They also have a longer average life span compared to horses, often easily making it to 30 years or more. They are very smart, and are considered wily or clever. They know all the tricks to play on their humans! This is what can make them less than ideal mounts for small children or beginners.

Ponies have a tougher digestive system than the horse, and are able to survive quite well on less-than-ideal forage. This makes it very easy to overfeed a pony, which can have serious effects. They are very strong for their size, able to pull loads much heavier than their horse counterparts. A pony can pull up to twice its own weight. They can carry 20% of its weight on its back, compared with 15–18% for an average horse.

They're built to be tough. Ponies have proportionally denser bones and shorter legs. They are hardy, and can withstand large variations in temperature due to having much thicker coats, manes, and tails. The hooves of a pony are also very tough and more dense than those of a horse, making them quite suited to rough terrain.

Horses tend to be more docile, and the larger the breed, the quieter their temperaments. They are generally more amenable to working long days or training for sport. Ponies are feisty and playful; they know how to get out of work very well. There is one thing that cannot be doubted about ponies, however. They are so darned cute!

A herd of furry Icelandic ponies doesn't mind the weather.

STORY: A BIG-HEARTED HORSE

Secretariat is known worldwide as having been one of the best race horses in the world. In 1973, this equine elite athlete won the Triple Crown of Thoroughbred racing which includes three races: the Kentucky Derby, the Preakness, and the Belmonts Stakes. Secretariat still holds the record for the fastest average speed overall at 37.8 mph, and the fastest track records for both the Derby and the Stakes.

Big Red was Secretariat's nickname, because he was a solid red-chestnut color. When Secretariat died in 1989 at the relatively young age of 19, veterinarians conducting a post mortem exam (after death) discovered that the horse's heart weighed almost 23 pounds. Not impressed? You should be—the average horse's heart weighs only about eight or nine pounds, meaning Secretariat's heart was about two-and-a-half times larger! That Big Red was a big-hearted horse.

3

HOW HORSES ARE BUILT

> *There is something about the outside of a horse that is good for the inside of a man.*
>
> — WINSTON CHURCHILL

Horses are complex creatures. They can be very big or quite small, yet both have lots of parts. Throughout this book we're going to use a lot of terms that refer to parts of a horse. Here we will take a look at the major parts of the horse—the ones most often referred to when discussing riding, training, working with, and caring for a horse.

MAJOR PARTS OF THE HORSE

The better you know the parts of the horse, the easier it is not only for you to talk about your horse, it's also easier to learn when you know what your instructors, veterinarians, or farriers are referring to. Sometimes, the placement of the parts can help you figure out how the horse uses them:

- Ears are set high up and can independently swivel around to determine where sounds are coming from and their distance. The ears also indicate where the horse's attention is focused.
- The eyes are set widely across the face and are quite prominent. This gives the horse an almost 360-degree field of vision, which helps it detect motion that could be predators.
- Long tails and manes help deter insects; a shake of the mane or swish of the tail readily, though temporarily, can shoo pests away. Long, flexible necks mean that horses can scratch itches almost anywhere on their bodies except the back, rump, and belly.
- Inside, the horse's reflexive muscles make it quite capable of quick actions to avoid danger, and the check ligament in the hind legs is what allows a horse to lock one leg in place so that it

can rest another and remain standing. This is why so many people think that horses sleep standing up.

The diagram below shows the main parts of the horse:

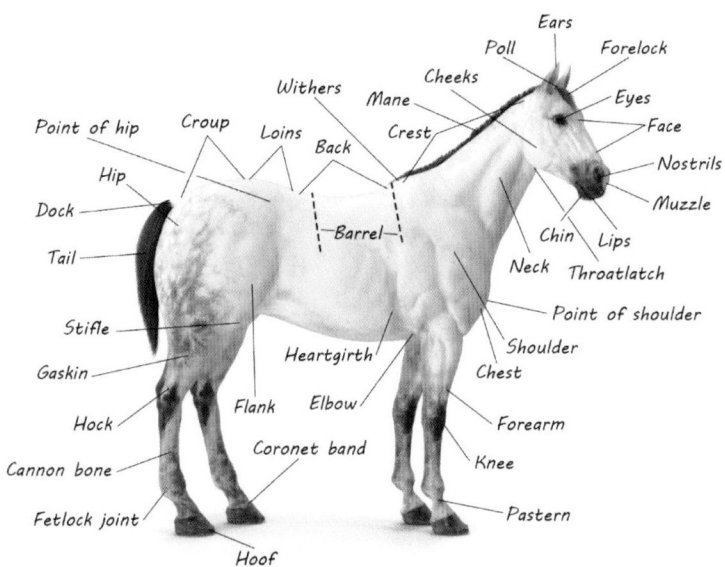

List of Parts from Nose to Tail

- head—chin, lips, muzzle, nostrils, face, cheeks, eyes, forelock, throatlatch, poll, ears
- neck—mane, crest
- front end—chest, shoulder, point of shoulder, elbow, withers

- front leg—forearm, knee, cannon bone, fetlock joint, pastern, coronet band, hoof
- body—back, barrel, heartgirth, loins, flank
- hind end—croup, hip, point of hip, dock, tail
- hind leg—stifle, gaskin, hock, cannon bone, fetlock joint, pastern, coronet band, hoof

You might have noticed that the legs are the same once you get past the big, middle joint. One easy way to remember those big joints is to think about how your knee bends. The horse's knee bends the same way as yours, that is, forwards. The hock is below the dock (tailbone) and in the back—all short words that end in "ck."

Some parts are easy to identify because they compare with our own, like the back, neck, chest, and face. Some are a bit trickier; we call the middle of the horse where the rib cage is the barrel, because it is shaped like one. A horse doesn't have a thigh, it has a gaskin. Try to find your own tricks for remembering all the different parts.

HIDDEN PARTS

Besides the internal organs, there are two other very important hidden parts to a horse: the teeth and the hooves. In the case of the hoof, all we see is the outside; we will look at the bottom and some of the vital interior parts. Horses have a diet quite different from ours, and their mouth and teeth have developed to be optimal for almost constant grazing. Let's peek inside.

The Hoof, Inside and Out

There is an old saying, "No hoof, no horse." What could that mean? Well, a horse is a big animal that stands on four relatively small feet. It's a truism because a horse cannot be ridden or used for work, war, or any other purpose if its feet are not in prime condition. Those hard but delicate feet need to be strong and healthy so that a horse can move easily and comfortably, and so that we can enjoy riding or driving them! Despite their tough exterior, the inside of a hoof is made up of complex parts including bones, ligaments, tendons, and soft tissue. All that inside one hoof!

One of your most important tasks in caring for your own horse will be to take care of those feet every day, and to make sure your farrier comes to trim and tend to them at least every eight weeks. Whether your horse is barefoot or wears shoes, regular care and maintenance will keep him happy and comfortable while at work or play.

List of Parts of the Hoof

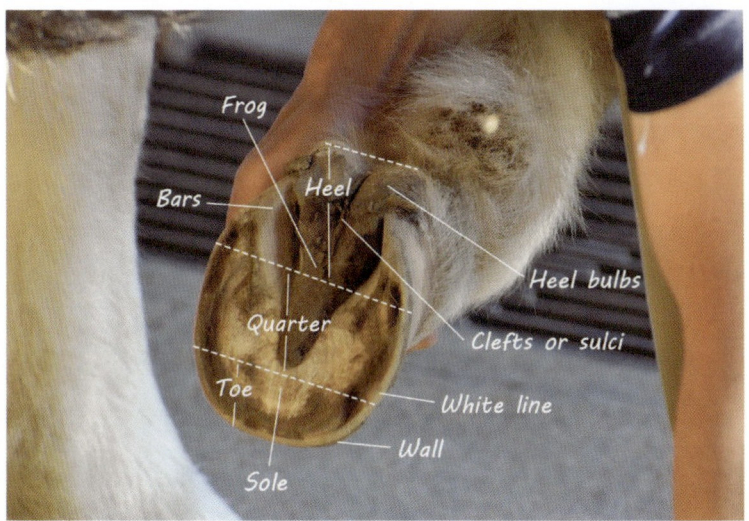

The outer hoof wall is not sensitive; it's like the ends of your own fingernails. It can be trimmed and nailed into without any discomfort to the horse. If your horse wears shoes, either lack of attention or a poor diet will make the wall begin to crumble, and the shoes will not stay on properly. Overgrown feet will also be a problem.

Hoof Maintenance by a Professional

A horse's hoof wall grows continuously. This is one reason that regular care by a professional farrier is so important. When the hoof wall grows too long, it can crack or break away down to sensitive inner tissue. If not tended to, shoes will get loose and come off, frequently taking chunks of the hoof with them. Toes that are allowed to grow too long can change the way a horse stands and moves. It can unbalance the horse, putting too much stress on other parts of the hoof or legs. It may also make him prone to stumbling, which is not safe for either the horse or its rider!

Make your farrier your new best friend!

A farrier fits a show to a horse's hoof before nailing it on.

Hoof Maintenance You Can Do

Horses walk over all types of ground: stony, muddy, manure-coated, and even snowy. Every day you will want to pick your horse's feet, whether or not you plan to ride. Regular cleaning will prevent bruises and abscesses from stones trapped in the hoof by dirt or mud. And those deep clefts on either side of the frog, or *sulci*, must be kept clean and free of manure and mud. If left for too long, that gunk could cause a serious fungal infection called *thrush*.

During the winter, it can be hard to get the packed snow and ice out of your horse's hooves. But it's necessary. There might be stones or muck hiding under that hard pack, and horses can develop large snowballs in their feet—especially if they have shoes on—that can quickly become treacherous. It's like walking in high heeled shoes with ice for soles.

When shopping for products to care for your horse, you may see a lot of oils and treatments to apply on the outer covering of the hoof. In general, all these products do is look pretty and make you feel like you are taking extra care of your friend. The reality is that they are not necessary, and over time can even start to ruin the hoof wall by keeping it either too damp and oily all the time, or by drying it out with harsh ingredients.

The best way to keep your horse's feet healthy top and bottom is to keep them regularly picked, ensure you're feeding a good, healthy balanced diet with lots of fresh water available, and by avoiding leaving your friend standing in wet, muddy areas for long periods.

Did You Know?

Just like a horse's teeth, the horse's hooves grow forever. This is one reason why your horse needs a visit from your farrier every two months at a minimum. We've learned that long toes on a horse can make shoes loose, contribute to tripping and stumbling, are more prone to chip and split, and set a horse off balance enough to damage the soft tissues, or tendons, muscles, and ligaments, in his legs.

But what happens if they don't get trimmed?

Neglected horses are found all the time with hooves that have grown so long, they actually began to curve back from the front towards the leg. They look a little like elf slippers with curled toes, but for the horse it is a dire situation. They can't walk, and the possibility for permanent damage inside the hoof is very real. Months and months of frequent, small trims from the farrier are often necessary to get the feet back to their proper shape.

Looking a Gift Horse in the Mouth

Horses' teeth are pretty amazing. After they lose their first teeth, or milk teeth, they develop molars and incisors just like we do. They use their incisors to tear grass and hay, then, using their tongue, move the food back to the molars for grinding. The lips and tongue do most of the work picking up fine foods, like grains. There are several unique features to a horse's teeth, however, that make them very different from ours. Once grown, our teeth are done; but, like their hooves, a horse's teeth continue growing for a very long time! Their natural diet of coarse grass helps keep those teeth worn down to an appropriate length and shape.

Today, we often keep our horses in stables without access to large pastures for grazing. Instead, we feed our horses grains and concentrates (grains mashed then steamed into small pellets) which don't wear down the teeth much. Having easy access to good quality hay helps with maintaining the balance between ease of feeding and proper tooth function; the coarse hay does a good job of keeping the teeth healthy.

The incisors of an older horse. You can clearly see the flat surfaces of those teeth and how they will meet. How do we know it's an older horse? The length of the teeth and the angle they have towards the front are two signs.

This photo shows how the incisors, or front teeth, meet almost perfectly to help rip and tear at grass or leaves—or bite an apple in half! You can also see the long gap without teeth, called the bars of the mouth, between the incisors and molars. This is where a bit rests in a horse's mouth.

If you look closely at the molars, you can definitely see how they have worn from years of eating—longer on the outside of the uppers on this side and on the inside of the lower teeth. On the other side, the lowers will be higher on the outside, and the uppers shorter. Can you guess why? Here's a hint: Read on to learn about the motion of the lower jaw when a horse chews.

Dentistry for Horses

Horses don't chew up and down like we do. Because horses grind their food, their jaws work in a continuous circular motion. That makes the surfaces of the molars work against each other from one side to the other, sliding across at an angle.

Over time, this sliding action can make the edges of the molars quite sharp—sharp enough to create sores and abscesses inside the cheeks. One way to know that a horse has tooth problems is by noticing signs of discomfort with the bit: cocking or tossing its head, avoiding contact with the bit by the reins, or hanging on one rein are all signs. Another indication the teeth need attention is that the horse can no longer properly eat. You might see clumps of partially chewed hay on the ground, or notice spilling grain out of its mouth. These issues can lead to weight loss in your horse, making yet another reason why it's a good idea to keep track of weight gain and loss.

An equine dentist or veterinarian can use a long file to smooth out those sharp edges, making your horse more comfortable while eating and when it has a bit in its mouth. This will also get rid of the cause of the sores, allowing them to heal. At least once a year, you should have your vet or an equine dentist examine your horse's teeth and mouth. They can find any injuries or sore spots, remove a cracked or loose tooth, and then file down any sharp edges.

Did You Know?

You can tell how old a horse is by looking at their front teeth! From the time they are born until they are quite old, a horse's teeth gradually change in length and shape. The top and bottom incisors (front teeth) of a horse generally meet perfectly. As they age, the teeth still meet, but grow longer and slanting forward, giving them an angle towards the lips.

When viewing the flat surface, young teeth are rounded and oval in shape, up to about age 11; that shape becomes more triangular and finally rectangular as the horse ages and the teeth lengthen and grow outwards. The biting surface starts out with a slight cup in the middle, which wears away by age eight.

Some people look at the groove that you see on the surface of the outermost upper incisor in the top photo. The length of that groove, called Galvayne's groove, can give you an approximate age of your horse. It appears when a horse is 9–10 years old, reaches halfway down the tooth at about 15 years, and runs top to bottom by around age 20. It then starts to recede: about halfway by age 25 and completely gone by age 30.

4

A HORSE OF A DIFFERENT COLOR

A good horse is never a bad color.

— MARK RASHID

Horses come in different shapes, sizes, and colors. There are various shades of black, brown, chestnut, and gray, of course, but there are also colors like gold, silver, blue, and even strawberry. They can be solid or spotted, with patches of colors, bright white markings, and a few even have stripes. A horse's coat color describes the main color of its body, and may include the colors of the legs, mane and tail.

BUT NO GREEN ONES?

Horses do come in a wide variety of colors, but they are not peacocks! Don't expect to see vibrant greens and pinks on your horse unless you put it there. What often makes a horse's color stand out is the contrast against white markings, or the shine of a healthy, well-cared for coat.

Let's start with the five basic coat colors:

- **Bay**—a base coat color of any shade of solid brown with black *points*: black lower legs, black mane and tail, and black around the ears and on the end of the nose.
- **Chestnut**—an overall body color of reddish brown ranging from bright orange to copper-red to muted orange-brown shades. The mane and tail are either matching or slightly lighter in color. A *sorrel* is a chestnut horse with a distinctly lighter mane and tail. *Liver-chestnut* is a variation that is a solid dark brown with a somewhat lighter mane and tail.
- **Black**—a true black coat with black skin and dark eyes. Very few breeds have true black horses. Horses with black coats that do not fade are called raven or jet-black. Black horses whose coats may fade in sunlight, as horses shed, or in areas that frequently get sweaty may develop areas that are very dark brown or red in places, but legs, mane, and tail remain black. Those horses are called fading-black or barn-black. Both fading and non-fading black horses are genetically black. If they have white markings, the skin beneath those may be pink.

- **Gray**—a white horse is actually gray, meaning they have black or dark skin and the eyes are brown. Shades can range from dark, almost black to pure white, with other variations, such as *dappled*, with large, lighter circles on the body, or *flea-bitten*, with lots of small reddish-brown freckles all over. Gray horses are most often born black or chestnut, but fade as they grow.
- **Brown**—brown coats are solid in color all over, but they may have white markings. They can be so dark as to appear almost black, but do not get as light as chestnuts. Chocolate and cocoa brown are common descriptions of this color. Unlike a liver-chestnut that sports a lighter mane and tail, a brown horse usually has a mane and tail that match the color of the coat.

Color Breeds

All of these colors have variations that cover a wide range and give us a rainbow of horses. Some horses are what are called "color breeds" meaning that it is their coat color rather than their type or breeding that gives them their name, regardless of their parent's being of a specific breed.

Here are some color breeds:

- **Palomino**—any shade of yellow from a pale, almost cream-like color to a deep dark gold. Palominos are a variant of chestnut. Their body color is solid, and the mane and tail are lighter than the coat. Very light, almost white manes and tails are called flaxen.
- **Pinto**—a combination of a base color, such as white, with large patches of color covering the body. Patches may be chestnut, brown, black, or gray. Pintos come in piebald, or white with black splotches, and skewbald, or white with any other color splotches and may be any breed. A paint horse must be at least 50% Quarter horse.
- **Appaloosa**—this breed is recognizable by its spots. The spots may be light on a darker base coat, or dark on a lighter coat. The spots are most commonly found as a blanket, an area covering the top of the rump behind where a saddle would go. Sometimes the spots are all over, and may be less distinct. A variation is the leopard appaloosa, which has a white coat with chestnut, black, or brown spots spread uniformly over its body.

A striking pinto horse, with three stockings, one sock, a star, and a race.

You can see why they are called leopard appaloosas.

Lots of Variations

Some coat colors are combinations of colors. Although this isn't a complete list, here are a few of the more common variations:

- **Roan**—this term refers to any solid coat color mixed evenly with white hairs. A strawberry roan is a chestnut horse with white hairs evenly mixed in. A blue or purple roan has a dark coat, black or brown, that gives a bluish tinge to the coat. A gray roan is possible, but it can be very difficult to tell whether it is really a gray or a gray pinto.
- **Buckskin**—the main body color is a light tan, with dark points: legs, mane, tail, ears and muzzle (tip of the nose). They may also have a darker stripe running down their back from the mane to the tail, known as a dorsal stripe.
- **Dun**—commonly confused with buckskin, dun horses may have a grayish or sandy-brown coat, or even a pale yellow one, with a very clear dorsal stripe. The mane and tail may not be dark. Often, dun horses have stripes near the tops of their legs. A variant of dun is grullo, a dun mixed with black, which generally appears as a dark gray roan with dark legs, mane, tail,

and muzzle. A dun may have a dark or black face mask, a dorsal stripe, and stripes on the legs. A dun horse must have one parent that is also dun.

Right, a grullo with a full mask. On the left is a paint with a bald face.

ALL THOSE WHITE MARKINGS!

The white patterns we typically see on a horse's face and legs are called markings. Made of white hair over mostly pink skin, these markings are generally differentiated by size, shape, and location on the horse's body.

Leg Markings

Horses may have leg markings that are so small you only know they are there because the hoof is a different color. Any time that pink skin or a white marking goes down into the hoof, all or part of it may appear whitish instead of dark gray. Markings may show up on only one leg, or up to all four. They might match, or could be different sizes on each leg.

Common leg markings are:

- **Stockings**–white leg markings that start at the hoof and continue up the legs and go above the big joint in the middle of the leg.
- **Socks or half-stockings**—white markings that go up the leg past the first joint (fetlock) above the hoof to below the big, middle joint (knee or hock).
- **Pasterns**—named for the area where it is found, a white pastern marking goes up to, but not above, the fetlock joint above the hoof.
- **Coronets**—here, the white stays below the fetlock joint, and may only go part-way around the leg.

Face Markings

One of the most striking features on a horse can be its face markings. Or they can be so small they are almost overlooked. They come in different shapes and sizes, but they are always white. We're going to start with the small and work our way up:

- **Snip**—a snip is an adorable tiny patch of white on the end of a horse's nose, between the nostrils or lower down on the upper lip. If one is found on the lower lip, then it is referred to as a chin or chin spot.
- **Star**—often shaped like a star or diamond, this is a patch of white between the horse's eyes or higher. It can be anywhere from a small dot of white to a flashy, big, white print. A star is contained; it doesn't cover the eyes or run down the length of the face.
- **Stripe or strip**—running from anywhere on the forehead above or below the eyes down toward the nose, this is a strip of white that may be continuous or interrupted for a short distance.
- **Race**—like a stripe, but thinner and more jagged in shape.
- **Blaze**—again like a stripe, but much wider. A blaze is still more or less centered in the front,

but extends beyond the nasal bone of the nose toward the eyes. The length may be as long as from under the forelock all the way down including the nose.

- **Bald Face**—essentially a blaze that is so wide it covers most of the front of the face. If it extends beyond the eyes and onto the cheeks, that horse will most likely have blue eyes, instead of brown, due to the change in the skin color.
- **Lip or chin**—If either the upper or lower lip has a white marking, it's simply called a lip or chin.

Combinations of facial markings are quite common. For example, a horse may have a star, and under that a stripe, and below that a snip. Or it could be just a star and snip, or a race and snip. You get the idea!

This foal may outgrow his beautiful blaze, which could shrink as his head grows, becoming a star, stripe, and snip.

A bold, bright star on a true black horse.

A good example of a bald face on this chestnut.

A show horse with a star, race, snip, and lower lip.

Even a white horse can have white markings, as shown by the large snip on the muzzle of this gray. There is even a bit of a lip, too.

STORY: A RESCUE TURNED CHAMPION

Snowman, a speckled-gray retired plow horse, was on a truck to be sold at auction, when he was purchased right off the trailer for $80. Rider and trainer Harry deLeyer saw something in the horse's eyes, and thought he would be perfect for his riding school in New York.

Snowman quickly became a favorite of the family and the school. During the week, all the students wanted to ride him, and on weekends he would carry the deLeyer children into the lake for a swim. But hard times were coming; the family had to reduce the herd. Snowman was sold to a very nice man down the road who promised to take good care of him.

The next day, the new owner called to say that the horse was missing! Since none of the fences were broken or gates open, it was assumed the horse had been stolen. Alarmed, Harry went outside, intending to go to the other farm, when he saw Snowman standing in his old paddock. The talented escape artist repeated the trick several times, despite being put into paddocks with higher and higher fences, before the owner gave him back to the deLeyers. He was too much trouble!

After his return, Harry began riding the horse more and more to see just how well the horse could jump. It turned out, not only could Snowman jump very high fences, he absolutely loved it! Harry and Snowman began going to horse shows, and quickly became a celebrated pair, winning many showjumping championships. Together, they—the Galloping Grandfather and the $80 Champion—won Horse of the Year two years in a row in 1958 and '59. Their amazing story was made into a popular book and later a full-length movie.

5

FEEDING YOUR HORSE

" *Beware the hobby that eats!*

— BENJAMIN FRANKLIN

Unlike people, horses were made to live outside. Their coats, hooves, digestive systems, and circulatory systems were all designed to withstand all sorts of weather conditions. Then we came along. We brought horses from the desert regions to cold climates, and heavy draft horses to the south. We started breeding them to have finer coats, specific colors, and other traits, and in doing so, took away some of that natural hardiness.

Regardless of those changes, what does remain true is that all horses (ponies and donkeys, too) require a few basic necessities, the same ones humans do: water, food, and shelter.

WATER

That might seem like an odd order to put things in; shouldn't food be first? Water is one of the most important nutrients that all animals—including you—need. Your horse should have 24/7 access to clean, unfrozen water. This could be buckets hung in a stall or shed, a tub or trough in the pasture or paddock, or some other variation. The important thing is to keep it clean by refreshing buckets daily or keeping troughs regularly cleaned out between fillings.

Automatic waterers are expensive to install, but are very useful in that they supply a constant supply of clean, fresh water, since they only refill as the horse is drinking. They require less cleaning than a trough or bucket, but the process may be trickier. Without regular maintenance and supervision, a broken waterer can result in wasting water from flooding or thirsty horses if the device is not flowing. A convenient fast running stream through your pasture is a great asset, however, you should still offer your horse water from a container; streams can carry parasites and infectious diseases.

While buckets and troughs might seem like a lot of work, one big advantage is that you can keep an eye on how much your horse is drinking. Horses need 10–15 gallons of water every day, and that's before they work hard and sweat a lot! If you notice your horse is drinking very little, he may become dehydrated. If he is drinking a lot without working, it may indicate health problems, such as kidney or liver issues. It can be a great early-warning sign.

FOOD

As briefly discussed above, a horse's diet is mainly roughage, meaning grass and hay. It can take up to five acres of grass to sustain one horse adequately. That same acreage might yield 600 hundred or more bales of hay each season.

Hay and Grass

There are many types of grasses, and they vary from state to state and region to region. Some contain more of certain nutrients than others, like proteins, carbohydrates, vitamins, and minerals. The fat in hay comes from the carbohydrates supplied by the sugars in the grass. This can vary not only among different types of grass, but also at different times of the year, and even different times of day! Good quality hay is free of dust and mold, and also toxic weeds and debris like old fruit or sticks.

Although we most often refer to all the green stemmed plants horses eat as grass or hay, a better term to use is roughage. Roughage, or forage, is what horses are designed to eat and process; just think about those cutting and grinding teeth. There are two main types of roughage: grasses and legumes. These can be supplied by grazing, or more commonly, by cutting and drying the roughage into hay. Hay is different types of grasses, legumes, or a mix of the two. The plants are allowed to grow tall, then just as they start to go to seed, they are cut close to the ground by a large mower pulled by a tractor. The grass is allowed to dry for two to three days, then raked and scooped up into a machine called a baler, also pulled by the tractor. A baler compresses hay into tight bunches—either rectangular or round—and ties it up with baling twine.

If kept in dry, airy storage conditions, such as in a hay loft, the bales will cure (dry completely) and keep for a long time. It's best to use hay within one year, as the nutrients fade over time. But as long as it smells sweet and is free from dust and mold, older hay is perfectly acceptable. Any hay you see that is particularly heavy as if wet, has a dark greenish or blackish patch that may be slightly damp, or has a white powder on it is moldy and should be discarded somewhere that horses can't get to it. Dusty hay is also bad for horses; however the older hay gets, the dustier it can become. Dust is a significant irritant and can cause serious breathing problems for your horse. If the hay still smells sweet and has a slightly green tinge to it, it may be fed out in the open air so that the dust can fly away or it can be wetted down prior to feeding.

Grasses

Depending on where you live, the grasses that grow there will be common to that area. A list of grasses that can be found in many locations with a temperate climate includes:

- bermuda grass
- brome
- fescue
- orchardgrass
- reed canary grass
- ryegrass
- timothy

Legumes

You already know about some legumes. These plants are all part of the same family as peas and beans, and include familiar plants like clover. A mix of legumes and hay will give your horse the best nutrition, whether in the pasture or as baled hay. A list of legumes commonly used for both is:

- clover–red and white
- alfalfa
- trefoil
- vetch

Soybeans are also a legume, and are commonly raised to feed cattle. Horses should never be fed raw soybeans or the green plants. Once it is dried, horses can benefit from the oils, fats, proteins, and amino acids in soybeans. It can be fed in the form of oil or meal.

Getting bales to feed. Note the nice green color of this grass hay.

Grains and Processed Foods

In addition to good hay, we may need to feed our horses more food to give them extra energy and to make up for nutrients that might be missing from their forage. Showhorses and other equine athletes may need more than hay and grass can provide. Pregnant and nursing mares and growing foals also benefit from nutritional supplementation. So we turn to grain and processed feeds to help keep our horses at their best. Even for pleasure horses, many people do not have sufficient pasture for their horses to meet their needs.

Grains such as oats, barley, and corn are common horse feeds. They are generally steamed and dried before being fed, though horses will happily eat corn right off the stalk, or wheat and barley grasses, if growing nearby. The process of steaming and drying means that those grains can be stored for longer periods without spoiling.

There is a science to creating the right balance of nutrients between straight grains and hay. One way to make this easier is to buy concentrates, or processed grains. During processing, a combination of grains is ground up and steamed. Then the mixture is pressed together to make small pellets, similar to rabbit food. In doing so, companies can combine a variety of ingredients and add special nutrients, such as vitamins, minerals, and extra fats. Grasses and legumes may be added, as well. This helps horses with limited access to grass or high-quality hay, and older horses who can no longer properly chew those tough forage stems.

A horse can be left out on grass all the time, as long as he has no special issues that may prohibit that. They can have hay in front of them at all times, too, with the same warning. But horses have very small stomachs, and cannot tolerate large amounts of grains or concentrates in one feeding. If overfed, they can develop a serious condition called *colic*—a very bad stomach ache that may require surgery or could even end the life of the horse.

For such a large animal, the stomach can only hold three to five quarts of food at a time, though trying to feed even that much at once will likely still cause issues. Breaking down the total amount and increasing the number of times per day that you offer food to three times, at the very least two, allows the horse to digest steadily.

Horses like a routine, so try to feed your horses at the same times every day. Being off by a little occasionally is fine, but skipping meals or feeding several hours late can make some horses very anxious. Irregular feeding also makes it harder to monitor how much they're being fed overall, which creates difficulties knowing when to make adjustments to their rations, and by how much.

Work with your veterinarian to put together a diet that works well for your horse. It will likely be a combination of roughage and concentrates. Be careful in deciding what to feed based on other people's experiences or what the grain bags say. It is easy to overfeed concentrates, or to feed the wrong type for your horse's needs. Always, always make sure that what you feed your horse is not moldy or dusty. Dispose of grains that smell sour, have a whitish or greenish coating, or that generate dust when handled.

HOW MUCH FOOD?

Putting together a horse's diet needs to take into account a lot of factors. The size and breed of the horse, how much exercise it is getting, access to hay and pasture, and the time of year will all determine the total amount you need to feed. In general, a horse should receive 1.5%–2.0% of its body weight every day, and most of that should be roughage. In summer, that percentage will be toward the lower end, and in winter, it will be higher. That means that an average horse weighing about 1,000 pounds should receive 15–20 pounds of "dry matter," or hay and grain, with at least 60–75% of that total in forage.

What's important is that your horse receives high-quality, nutritious food and maintains an overall good body condition. Body condition scores range from "very thin" to "very fat" and ideally you want your horse's condition in the mid-range. Along with monitoring weight, a body condition chart will help you keep track of your horse's condition. On this chart, scores range from one to five; other charts may use a different range. The goal is to visualize a baseline "ideal" condition, and see how much, if any, your horse varies from that.

Body Condition	Score	Description
Poor/Very thin	1	Horse appears emaciated; withers, ribs, tailhead, point of buttocks, hip, and shoulder all prominent; spine sunken on either side
Thin/ Moderately thin	2	Ribs and spine somewhat visible; withers still prominent; neck appears thin; tailhead and points less prominent or slightly covered
Moderate	3	Back is level; ribs can be felt but not easily seen; fat around tailhead appears; neck, barrel and hind quarters blend smoothly
Moderately fleshy	4	Shallow crease down the back may appear; ribs harder to feel through fat; tailhead, withers, and shoulders have a clear layer of soft fat.
Very fleshy/fat	5	Clear crease down back; difficult or impossible to feel ribs; fat around tailhead very soft; areas behind withers and shoulders filled with fat; thickening of the neck; inner thighs touch due to fat

Did You Know?

The American Quarter horse is the most popular breed of horse in the US. They are sturdy, smooth-gaited, and generally calm and friendly. They are the favorite horse in a variety of equestrian sports and activities, including ranching, games, show horses, jumping, gymkhana, children's mounts, lesson horses, trail riding, and rodeo games.

With a mixture of Mustang, Spanish, and later, Thoroughbred bloodlines, Quarter horses were bred to be versatile for work and play. And play they did! The name "Quarter horse" comes from their ability to run one quarter of a mile very fast. In fact, at that distance, running at speeds up to 44 mph, they are the fastest animal on earth!

Unfortunately, some Quarter horse bloodlines have become susceptible to certain health issues. One of those is having metabolic problems, meaning trouble utilizing and processing nutrients, such as fats and carbohydrates. A specially-formulated diet can help these horses thrive. If not addressed, this metabolic syndrome can cause obesity and severe lameness.

6

BARN MANAGEMENT 101

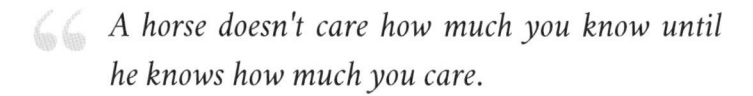

> *A horse doesn't care how much you know until he knows how much you care.*
>
> — PAT PARELLI

In the last chapter we learned all about the types of feeds and the feeding process. Now let's look at shelter. Whether your horse is a backyard pet or a superstar in the show ring, shade, a windbreak, and shelter from rain or snow are essential. Shelters vary from a simple run-in shed to a fancy barn with large stalls. Even a stand of trees can offer adequate protection from wind and rain.

One thing that all forms of shelter need is proper management. This includes keeping the structure clean

—free from manure and standing water or urine—and in good repair, with no loose boards or nails for horses to find and injure themselves on (unfortunately they are experts at this!).

A PADDOCK AND RUN-IN

A run-in is pretty much what it sounds like. It's a three-walled structure that allows horses to freely walk in or out of the open fourth side. Your run-in can sit inside the paddock or be a part of the fence line. Whichever works easier for you to manage the space well. Sheds need to be tall enough to allow a horse to raise its head without hitting the ceiling, and roomy enough so they can easily turn around. Although some horses are best buddies and don't mind standing hip to hip, it is always best to provide a minimum of eight square feet of area per animal of average size. This will help ensure that a bossy boots horse doesn't keep less aggressive herd mates out.

The roof of the shed may extend beyond the inside, allowing horses to have shade, a break from the wind, or partial shelter from weather without going into the shed completely. Your run-in doesn't need to be its own freestanding structure, either. It could be one end or portion of an existing barn or other building that offers the same protections. Or it could be simply a roof built off of another building. As long as the structure is sound, and the space for the animals is safe, this is often the easiest option. Run-in sheds and similar set-ups are a very healthy way to keep horses. They are able to move around freely and to seek shelter when they want it, without being confined to a stall.

Two horses living in a pasture with a roomy run-in shed. The pasture is surrounded by a sturdy and beautiful wood rail fence.

Cleanliness

Regardless of the type of structure, keeping the area picked free of manure daily is important. Since you are already making sure that there is clean water and good food twice a day, you can make bringing a manure fork and wheelbarrow or muck tub with you a part of that routine. You can add bedding to a shed or shelter if you wish, though keeping it clean and dry is most important. Often, though, straw or shavings put into sheds is easily blown or kicked out and can be wasteful. Bedding will also make it a little more difficult to keep clean; on the plus side, it will help absorb any moisture and will soak up pee.

If the ground around the shed does not drain well, this can be a big problem. It is worth investing in grading and gravel to offer the horses a dry place to stand out of mud and urine. Remember how important it is to take good care of those hooves? Standing around in mud and yucky stuff will definitely ruin a horse's feet, and is a prime situation for the development of thrush!

If it is wet out, keep the hay as high and dry as you can, and put feed grain in tubs or pans to keep it off the ground. You may need to attach these to the walls if your horse likes to play with his feed pan when it's full of grain. However you choose to set up your water, it should be easily accessible by both you and the horses.

BOX STALLS

A stall is a space inside a barn with four walls. The most common stalls are called boxes, and are large enough for the horse to easily turn around or lie down in. Sizes vary, but try to have a minimum space of 10 feet by 10 feet; however, 12 by 12 is better. Stalls require the same management that sheds do, including removal of manure and urine at least once a day, access to a clean water supply, and a clean area to eat from. This could just be a designated corner of the floor for hay, with a tub for grain on the wall.

Since the horse is not free to go outside, stalls require bedding like shavings or straw. The bedding alleviates issues created by standing in manure and from breathing in the smell of urine all day, also offering your buddy a dry place to sleep. Any barn with stalls needs to have good ventilation. Odors and moisture can build up in an enclosed space, and your horse won't be able to move away from the source. Making sure that stall walls are open near the top, using ventilation fans, and keeping doors and windows open whenever possible are good management solutions for keeping the air fresh.

Again, safety and preventing injuries are paramount to a well-run barn. Door latches and hardware should be horse-safe, floors relatively level with no holes, and wall boards in good repair. Check stalls regularly for loose or protruding nails and rusting or wiggly hinges and latches.

Offering your horse in-and-out access from his stall to a paddock, or letting your horse get out of his stall for the day or night into an area with a shed gives your equine partner the best of both worlds.

A happy horse hanging out in his box stall, one of many in this barn.

This horse can decide to stay in his stall or go out to his paddock.

TYPES OF FENCING

Around your shed or next to your barn is something vital to the safety of your horses. It's a fence! Good fencing is a necessity while bad fencing is inexcusable. Your fence needs to be both horse-safe and horse-proof. While it doesn't need to be fancy, it does need to be made of something your horse will respect. Every type of horse fencing has its pros and cons. You will want to consider your needs, site, and cost, as well as your horse's personality.

Electric Fencing Options

Electric wire fences are the most common type of fencing. There are different types, so make sure you choose something horse-safe. High-tensile strength wire has some good points, but is not generally considered a good choice for horses. It resists stretching out and sagging very well, won't break if a horse leans on it, and can be easily maintained. However, that same strength means it won't break easily if a horse gets caught up in the wire. Horses do tend to reach over, under, and through fences, and can run and play pretty hard. A face, neck, or leg that gets caught in high-tensile wire can get seriously hurt precisely because the wire is too strong; it will cut your horse badly long before it ever breaks.

Softer wire, such as galvanized steel or aluminum, have the opposite pros and cons. They will both break under pressure, and galvanized steel resists rusting; on the other hand, they will stretch easily, requiring a bit more attention to keep them taut and safe.

Fiberglass fencing comes in spools that look like either thin rope or flat tape. The fiberglass has thin wires running through it that conduct electricity. Many people like this kind of electric fencing because it is more visible than plain wire. On the down side, it has the same super-stretch factor that can get a horse tangled or injured.

Keeping It Hot

Electricity is what makes the above kinds of fences work. Don't worry, if your horse gets stung they will not be hurt, just very alarmed. A good fence charger, whether battery operated or plugged into a safe, protected outlet, can make the difference between peace and loose horses. Some horses are smart enough to test a wire fence with their whiskers; if it isn't live, they may just stroll right through it.

Make sure the charger you use is powerful enough for the total distance of wire used. For example, if you have a three-strand fence, you will need a charger that will do the whole distance of the perimeter, times three. For areas far away from the barn, an alternative to using batteries is to get solar chargers. These also have a battery; however, it keeps itself charged whenever the sun is out, and keeps the fence running all night and on cloudy days. They can last years before they need replacing.

Wooden Fences

Wooden planks or rails can make for a beautiful fence that will last a long time. They require sturdy wooden posts (there are some all fiberglass versions of posts and rails) to keep the boards up, and horses love to lean and chew on them. Putting strands of electric wire on the inside or above each board can help prevent this behavior. Be advised that a habitual fence chewer can go through a 2x6 inch board in a matter of hours!

Posts

There are several types of posts for any of the above choices. They all require plastic or ceramic insulators to hold the wire; that way, the power can keep running, and not get grounded out by the posts.

T-posts are heavy-duty metal posts that can be relatively easily pounded into the ground. They are fairly sturdy, and easy to straighten and reset or move as needed.

Fiberglass posts are easy to put in with a regular hammer, but wear gloves! The fiberglass can splinter, giving you nasty slivers in your hands. Fiberglass posts are very popular for creating smaller, temporary paddocks.

Wooden posts can be either round or square, and may be chemically treated to last a long time underground. Cedar is a good choice for wood that keeps well and is non-toxic. While requiring the most work to put in, they are by far the sturdiest posts. Set below the frost line, they won't shift too much. However, they are not considered easily moveable. Once they are crooked, they need to be reset, and if broken, they need to be pulled out and replaced. Hard, rocky ground is not a good place to set deep wooden posts. But they are the only posts that will hold up heavy wooden rails.

A Basic Barn Checklist

As you create the space your horse will be in, you will need tools for maintenance, and also good ways to set up everything you need. We will get to direct horse care soon! The list that follows is for care of the barn area and feeding of the horse:

- **Pitchfork or manure fork:** to pick up manure and wet shavings or soiled hay.
- **Rake:** to clean up any spoiled hay and rake bedding smooth.
- **Muck tub or wheelbarrow:** to move all the gross stuff from the paddock to the manure pile.
- **Water system:** hoses, automatic shut-offs, troughs, or buckets.
- **Feeding:** tub or bucket on ground or on wall for grain; rack for hay if ground is wet.
- **Broom:** to keep barn floors clean and remove cobwebs regularly, especially from light fixtures.
- **Tool box:** Hammer, drill/driver, nails and screws, pry bar, saw, spare screw eyes and snaps for hanging items.
- **Metal trash cans:** 20–30 gallon size for rodent and waterproof storage of grain, plus bungies to secure the lid.
- **Dry storage area:** not accessible to horses for hay, blankets, tools, equipment, etc.
- **Fence supplies:** spare wire or fence boards to quickly fix broken fences.
- **List of emergency numbers** including veterinarian, farrier, fire, and ambulance.

This aisle is kept safe and tidy while being cleaned.

STORY: THE MYSTERY OF A KIDNAPPED RACING STAR

An unsolved crime in Ireland in 1983 was the kidnapping of the champion racehorse Shergar. The bay stallion was the most famous and valuable horse in the world at that time. He'd won the Epsom Derby (Ireland) only two years before by an amazing 10 lengths. This winning distance still holds the record for the more than 200-year-old race. In that same year, Shergar went on to four more major derby wins and was named European Horse of the Year.

On a late winter evening in 1983, two armed men came to the residence of Shergar's trainer, where the horse was being stabled. The men demanded that the trainer's son, who opened the door, take them to the horse. They told him that they planned to kidnap the horse with his help, and demanded $3 million dollars for Shergar's safe return.

At the stable, a horse trailer was ready to go, and several more armed men in masks were standing by. When the trailer was loaded, they put the trainer's son in the truck with them and drove off. Several miles down the road, the kidnappers dumped the man at the side of the road. He ran back to call first his father, then Shergar's vet, explaining what had just happened. After that, he called the police. Many people at the time said the delay in notifying the police of the event was what allowed the bandits to get away.

Although the kidnapper's got in touch several times, no ransom was ever agreed on, and the actual fate of Shergar remains unknown. Most experts and investigators say they believe the horse was killed, and his body either dumped into a peat bog, where it would sink away forever, or into the ocean.. Yet, to this day neither the remains of the horse nor the kidnappers have ever been found.

YOUR CHANCE TO HELP OTHER RIDERS – AND THEIR HORSES!

"A horse doesn't care how much you know until he knows how much you care. Put your hand on your horse and your heart in your hand."

— PAT PARELLI

I know you care about horses – if you didn't, you wouldn't be here reading this now.

By this stage in the book, you're bursting with new knowledge and preparing to take care of a horse and form a strong relationship with it. You want to make sure that the horse is healthy, cared for, and living the best life possible as much as you want to ride it and love it.

I know this because all animal lovers are the same – we care for the well-being of our animals as much as we care about the joy they bring us.

That's why I wanted to write this book for you – so that you would have all the knowledge you need to take care of your new friend. But I know you don't just care about *your* horse – you care about *all* horses… and this is your chance to make sure other horses out there get the same care and understanding that yours does.

All it takes is a few minutes of your time…

By leaving a review of this book on Amazon, you'll let other young horse enthusiasts know where they can find the information they need to care for and understand their horses.

Simply by letting other readers know how this book has helped you and what they'll find inside it, you'll show them where they can find all the guidance they need… and in doing so, you'll make sure their horse has the best possible chance at a happy and healthy life.

Thank you so much for your help. Horses are beautiful creatures, and I want to make sure as many young riders as possible have everything they need to take care of them.

Scan the QR code below for a quick review!

7

DAILY HORSE CARE

> *Grooming: the process by which dirt is transferred from your horse to you.*
>
> — ANONYMOUS

Fencing? Check. Shelter? Check. Water set-up? Check. Food? Hay and grain, check and check. Is that all? Of course not! We haven't touched our horse yet, other than maybe a pat while we feed it. You wash your face, brush your teeth and hair, and maybe even shower every day, right? Well, your horse deserves the same treatment, except in the horsey-version.

Regular visits from the farrier and vet will be scheduled, for the most part, so they are not an everyday occurrence. You will need to set up a schedule with your farrier for a trim or re-shoeing at six to eight week intervals. You will see your veterinarian at least twice a year, to make sure your horse stays up-to-date with his vaccines, including rabies and tetanus, and to check his manure and treat him for internal parasites. Good feed with a proper diet will keep him healthy on the inside. Yet there are important frequent tasks at hand to make sure our horses stay healthy on the outside as well.

SAFETY FIRST

Whether you're busy feeding, cleaning water buckets, or getting your horse from the pasture to groom and ride, keeping yourself and your friend safe are the first order of business.

There are hundreds, or so it seems, of safety rules to follow when working around horses. Each one has a solid reason for existing to prevent injury. Once explained they all make perfect sense, yet, being the irrational creatures we can be, we can still assume that they don't apply to us. Thoughts about safety and its protocols will appear throughout the rest of the book, but here are a few to get started with:

- Wear proper footwear around the barn and when working with horses. Getting stepped on is no joke, and can easily rip the skin off your foot or break bones. Around the barn, there is always a risk of stepping on an errant nail from an old horse shoe or a bit of wire from the fence.
- Never approach a horse directly from the front or rear, but instead at an angle. Horses cannot see directly in front of their noses or behind their rumps.
- Keep both your voice and your movements calm; avoid sudden actions or loud noises, as these may alarm your friend.
- Maintain a tidy barnyard. Make sure that wheelbarrows, forks and rakes, hoses, buckets, and other tools are always stored safely away, rather than lying around. These create a hazard for both you and your horse. A neat barn is a safe barn!
- When working with your horse, keep a well-fitted halter on him. A halter is a simple type of headgear—like a bridle without a bit, but looser—used to lead your horse from paddock to barn or tie him in a safe way for grooming.
- The lead rope attached to the halter should be carried in your right hand just below the snap,

and the extra in one loose loop in the left hand, so that you are walking on your horse's left side. Don't let the rope drag, as this can create a domino effect that begins when either you or your horse trips. This startles the horse. Maybe you get knocked to the ground. That startles the horse again—while you are down—which might get you hurt. It will also likely end up with the horse free and dragging the lead, which the horse thinks is a snake chasing it, which startles the horse, and so on. You get the picture, right?

Wrapping the rope around your hand or arm carries potentially frightening consequences, too. If the horse *balks*, *shies*, or *spooks*, and tries to run away, that rope wound around your hand isn't going to unwrap, it's going to tighten up immediately. Not only can this hurt, and possibly break your hand, if the horse continues to pull, it will pull you over. If the horse then runs away, you will get dragged along behind it, and not in a fun way.

- When leading, stay next to the horse just ahead of his shoulder, and look where you want to go. Horses understand our body language much, much better than we understand theirs. If we

are looking at them, they don't know where we want them to go. It's also a good way to accidentally pull your horse onto your own feet.
- The left side, also called the near side, is as a rule the side on which you will lead, mount and dismount your horse. You will also bridle him from that side, and start saddling him on the left, too. All horses are trained this way. Many don't mind which side you are on, but to be safe, when working with an unfamiliar horse, stick to the left, so he is in your right hand.

GROOMING

Grooming is the process of cleaning your horse's coat, hair, and feet. There are several steps involved that use simple tools to get the job done. The idea is to go over every inch of your horse to achieve these goals:

- Check for sores, cuts, or other issues.
- Remove mud, dirt, and loose hair from the skin and coat.
- Work to keep dander down by encouraging the oils in the skin.
- Spend quality time with your horse.
- Keep the mane and tail brushed and free from debris like burdocks.

- Pick the feet to remove mud, manure, and stones, and prevent soreness.
- Get an overall sense of how your horse is looking and feeling that day.

Grooming is not merely about making your horse look pretty; it has practical purposes. You'll know if your horse is beginning to have skin issues, such as *rain rot* if you have your hands on him every day. Even if you just notice that your friend is feeling a bit down, their eyes less bright, or perhaps they are just a tad too frisky, you are gaining valuable information. So let's get grooming!

Have your horse safely tied or in a confined area like a stall. If your horse doesn't stand quietly, you can quick-tie him in the stall in such a way that you can easily release him should it become necessary. Keep your bucket of grooming equipment close by, but not underfoot.

It's a good idea to start with picking the feet. If your horse has an injury to its hoof, sole, or lower leg, doing the feet first lets you know right away if some extra care is needed for a wound or the possibility of lameness. If he has a loose or missing shoe, you'll know that you need to call the farrier. In either case, a ride might not be possible that day, so it's better to find out sooner rather than later.

Picking feet

Using a tool called a hoof pick, stand next to your horse's shoulder and front leg facing the rear end. While bending at the waist (not squatting or kneeling), run your hand down the leg. When you reach the pastern, lean against the horse's side if they haven't already shifted their weight away from you. Be ready to catch the hoof as it's lifted off the ground. Some horses do this readily, and some may need more of a push, and a pull upward on the fetlock joint. Once up, grasp the hoof firmly in one hand, making sure it is well-supported. You should be cupping the hoof wall (hard part), not the pastern or fetlock (hairy parts).

With your free hand, grasp the hoof pick with the tip pointing down and away from the sole. Starting at the corners near the heels, dig firmly into the grooves (sulci) and move the pick away and diagonally forward toward the toe.

When the grooves are clean, pick the rest of the sole to remove any packed dirt or stones until you see something that looks slightly flaky and white; this indicates you've reached the bottom of the foot.

Watching your toes, gently slide your hand back up the leg until you either place the toe on the ground or the horse takes his foot from you; don't just drop the hoof suddenly.

Move to the hind leg of the same side and repeat. This time, when the horse starts to raise his foot, take another step or two back, closer to the tail, to help him stretch his leg and make it easier for you to see the sole of the hind foot. Repeat the process on the other side. Step one is done!

The proper technique for picking out a hind hoof. Note the hoof is held a little farther back than the tail.

Currying

A curry comb is an oval piece of plastic or rubber with blunt teeth on one side. Some are rigid, while some are quite flexible. When used in a circular motion while applying pressure, it can remove mud and loose hair from the coat, and also raise dirt and dander up off of the skin, bringing it to the surface. The idea is to massage your horse from: right behind its head all the way back to the buttocks; on top of the back, over the barrel, and under the belly; and down the legs as far as the knee and hock. Although he might look dirtier than when you started, this is a necessary step in grooming. When the curry gets filled with dirt or hair, simply tap it against a hard surface to clean it out before continuing.

Some horses are more sensitive than others. Thin-skinned types may prefer a soft, flexible rubber curry with short teeth, and less pressure. Tougher horses may love a stiff plastic curry rubbing and scratching them all over. Your horse will let you know what it prefers. Most horses do not like to have their faces or lower legs curried at all. Those areas do not have much flesh or fat on them, so it can be irritating. Avoid the temptation to run your hand over the coat after currying, as this will simply push the dirt and dander back in toward the skin.

Brushing: Dandy Brush First

The dandy brush, or hard brush, is used next. The bristles on a dandy brush are fairly stiff. Starting right behind the head again, this time you will work in short, firm, flicking strokes, following the direction of hair growth. This brush is designed to flick away all the dirt and dander the curry comb brought to the surface. Use it everywhere you used the curry. If your horse will tolerate it, you can go down the leg toward the hoof.

A young horseman uses a dandy brush on their horse.

Brushing: Body Brush Second

The body brush has much softer bristles. It is sometimes called a finishing brush. Use this brush everywhere on your horse including the face, ears, and lower legs to remove surface dust. Run your hand across the bristles from time to time to remove excess dust; you don't want to make your horse dustier than when you started.

The soft bristles of the body brush help remove surface dust from the coat and give it a shine.

Mane and Tail Comb

While you can use a hard brush or plastic curry to comb your horse's mane and tail, a regular hairbrush does a fine job, and can be kept just for that purpose. Some horse owners prefer to pick out the mane and tail with just their fingers, keeping the hair tangle-free without breaking and damaging the strands.

Shedding Blade

This is a handle tool, often a long, flexible metal strap with one smooth edge and one serrated edge. The smooth edge can be used to remove excess water, and the serrated side is great for helping your horse shed his winter coat or to remove dried mud.

Bathing, Braiding, and Other Extra Touches

Aside from regular basic grooming, there are many other ways you can pamper and attend to your horse. Many owners love to spend time with their horses this way.

Bathing

Horses in nature don't need baths. But giving your horse an all-over soapy bath is a great way to put an extra shine on the coat, get the skin thoroughly clean, and remove buried sweat and grime. Only use a mild, non-toxic shampoo, and be sure to keep it away from the eyes, ears, and nose. Rinse thoroughly, as leftover soap can make a horse itchy or give them a rash. Use warm water; some horses may not object to cold water, but most will be very happy if the water is at least 70 degrees Fahrenheit.

If your horse gets sweaty when you ride, be sure to hose or sponge off the sweaty areas, and scrape away the excess water. This removes the salt from the coat in order to keep it softer and help prevent bleaching from the sun.

Braiding

A horse's mane and tail can be braided in many ways and for a variety of reasons. Horses with long manes may get a french braid or running braid to help keep it tidy and out of the way while riding, or to spruce him up for a horse show. Shorter manes might be braided with many small braids in a row, then tucked up along the crest of the neck.

Different horse sports and breeds use different types of braiding techniques. In Hunter/Jumper sports, the mane is shortened to about 4 in. in length, and a series of 30–40 very small braids are tied tight to the crest. It is a lovely way to show off your horse's neck, however it is very time consuming and takes practice to get it looking great.

In dressage, fewer, wider braids are used. This requires a slightly longer mane. Wide, simple braids are made, then folded under themselves and tied at the top of the neck. Some people refer to these as "Dutch braids." There are around 9–15 braids along the neck for dressage.

Some breeds are usually kept with long manes, such as Morgans, Arabians, Lusitanos, and Andalusians. A running 3-part braid to one side of the crest is a quick, beautiful method. Making the running braid in four parts can keep the braids more secure. Double-braids are two braids side-by-side along the very top of the crest.

You can braid a horse's tail from the top of the dock, or top of the tailbone, all the way down to about half the length of the tail's skirt. This makes an elegant look for the show ring, and also helps show off his hind-end muscles. Or you can tie the tail up in a mud-knot, or a braid of the skirt only that is then wrapped around the dock and tied up tightly using nothing but the hair. The mud-knot keeps the tail out of the mud and free from twigs and burdocks.

There are so many ways to style your horse's mane and tail. It's fun to try them all.

Clipping

If you plan on working your horse year-round, you may choose to clip his coat in the colder months to prevent overheating while working, and to allow sweat to dry in order to be brushed away. There are many ways to clip a horse; just be aware that if you take hair away, you'll need to substitute it with blankets to keep him warm.

You can also clip the excess long hair around the hooves and fetlocks, and from under the jaw to maintain a very neat and tidy appearance. Some people clip the whiskers found on the muzzle, too, but this is generally no longer recommended. Horses need and use their whiskers for lots of things!

Some older horses with metabolic issues lose the ability to shed in summer, so they may need to be completely body-clipped when the weather gets warm. Be sure to have a light blanket or sheet if the nights get chilly when he is first shaved.

STORY: NOT AS FAMOUS AS DAD

There are so many well-known horses in Thoroughbred racing circles. Secretariat, Bold Ruler, American Pharaoh, and Seattle Slew, to name a few. There was Seabiscuit, the small horse with a crooked leg who took the race world by storm, winning the Kentucky Derby in 1937. Rich Strike was an 80:1 longshot when he won the Derby in 2022. Man o'War is still considered one of the greatest racehorses in history. The stallion won 20 races out of 21 starts, and though he never ran in the Kentucky Derby, he won both the Preakness—upsetting the favorite—and the Belmont Stakes—setting a racing record when he won by 20 lengths—the other two legs of the Triple Crown. In 1920, Babe Ruth and Man o'War both were awarded Athlete of the Year by the New York Times.

But have you heard about Man o' War's son, Battleship? Battleship was an American racehorse who began his career as a flat racer. Following an injury, he was purchased by Mrs. DuPont Scott of Virginia in 1931. Dupont had him put into steeplechase training rather than flat racing. He entered his first races in 1933; in 1934, he was entered into and won the American Grand National, the most prestigious race for steeplechasers in the country.

Ms. DuPont shipped the horse to England, planning to enter him in the 1937 Grand National, possibly the most famous steeplechase race in the world. That's the race featured in the book and movie National Velvet. Another injury, this time a bowed tendon, kept his training slow. Many trainers and sportswriters in England didn't think the small horse—ony 15.1 hands—had a chance in the Grand, especially after recovering from such an injury.

But, in 1938, Battleship was entered into the Grand National. In a photo finish, he won the race, beating the previous year's champion Royal Mail. Battleship was the first and only horse to win both the American Grand National and the Grand National (in England). Way to go, son!

THE MIND OF THE HORSE

> *In horsemanship, the task lies entirely with the rider to become more horse-like, not for the horse to become human.*
>
> — ERIK HERBERMANN

What do horses think? Why do they let us ride them? How come they behave the way they do? Are they communicating with us, or with each other?

Those are all very important questions. You will never be much more than a passenger on a horse until you understand more about him and how he interprets the world around him.

HOW TO READ A HORSE

You don't have to be a horse-whisperer or animal communicator to read your horse. With a lot of observation and a little practice, you will be able to detect changes in your horse's mood; a skill that will allow you to anticipate what his next actions may be. One fantastic way to learn how horses communicate non-verbally is to watch a group of horses throughout the day. Can you tell who the boss is? Which one is the low man on the totem pole? With some, it can be quite easy to tell, but many horses are very subtle when they "talk" to each other.

Watching a herd can give you a very good idea of the dynamics of the group. Who is in charge and are they nice about it? Horses rely on herd dynamics for their own safety and survival. Notice the expressions and actions—do they pin their ears and charge, or just threaten with a shake of the head and neck. Some horses only need to wrinkle their nostrils to let others know to keep back. Others are threat and action at the same time, with a snake and snarl, a charge with teeth bared, and then a quick spin to get ready to kick out with the hind legs.

Try putting out three flakes of hay in a large area with four horses. Watch who actually gets to eat, and who does not. Is there one that chases others from pile to pile, or do they settle down and just eat? It is often the case that the boss will pick the best pile, the second down gets the next, but may run the others around a bit first, and the next down gets the last pile. Some horses may share with number four, and that indicates a mild-mannered, docile temperament. On the other hand, that number three horse may continue to chase the number four horse away from the area, even though that means neither of them get to eat. A good rule to follow if spreading hay out in a paddock is to put out one or two more piles than there are horses, and to try to spread them well apart and in a rough circle.

What is this horse thinking? His ears-back expression shows he may be annoyed.

Facial Expressions and Other Physical Signs

Let's start with the head. What can a horse's face and head tell us? The most common detail people are taught is to watch the ears. When a horse's ears are pinned back, that's a sign of anger and possible aggressive defensive action. When they are pricked up and forward the horse is interested or content. Similar actions in a horse's expression can mean different things.

More on Ears

There are many variations to ears being back, for example. Yes, when the ears are pinned flat back against the neck, that is a clear sign the horse is unhappy about something. It could be another horse's approach, or the over-tightening of the girth on a saddle. It can also be a bad habit; horses that show aggressive tendencies are often reacting to previous negative experiences. If a horse had a sore back with a poorly fitting saddle that hurt them, or if the rider always tightened the girth too much too fast, it makes sense for them to react in a grumpy way. Some horses, even with their discomfort fixed or a new, more careful rider can keep reacting even in the absence of the trigger that they hated in the past. As a good horseman, it is your responsibility to try to figure out what is making the horse upset.

Ears firmly pricked up can be either positive anticipations, such as seeing you walk to the paddock with apples, or potentially negative ones, like an alert that something scary may be about to happen. In the first instance, that happy horse will keep looking at you, perhaps bobbing its head and nickering in greeting. In the second, if you notice the horse is blowing hard through its nose, and moving its head in a roughly circular pattern, they are sizing up a potential threat.

This can have two distinct outcomes: One, the horse decides the threat is real (to them, not you) and quickly spins away to create distance and get ready to flee—they may stop and assess again from farther away. Two, the horse realizes it's not a threat and will either approach and investigate or ignore the object all together.

Head and Teeth Threats

Teeth bared or snapping is a definite sign of aggression or defensiveness. If the action is directed at you, it is something you do not want to tolerate, but neither do you want to get mad at the horse for it. Wrinkling one nostril can be a sign, even before pinning an ear or two back or swinging the head.

Many horses threaten by pinning their ears and turning their mouth toward you as if to bite, though they won't act on it. It is their way of letting you know that whatever is going on is not appreciated. While you don't want to tolerate threats from your horse, since they may eventually turn into the real thing, it's your job to notice and change your behavior so the horse no longer feels the need to make the threat. Again, old habits die hard, as the saying goes, so your horse may continue making faces even if you do everything right. That's when your relationship with your horse can make all the difference. We'll talk about trust later on.

Neck Moves

Snaking of the neck often goes along with pinned ears, and is a warning to another horse to stay away. If the approaching horse is of higher rank, this won't be an effective tool. If the horse is of lower rank, then they hopefully get the message and leave space. If they don't, the dominant horse will escalate their behavior until threats and warnings become actions.

Horses will raise and lower their heads if they need to size something up. Depth perception, the ability we have to determine how close or far away an object is and then estimate its size, is not a horse's strong suit. This is a totally non-aggressive behavior; by moving their heads, they change the way their eyes see things, and can combine the information to help them decide if the thing is near or far, safe or dangerous.

Hind End Actions

The front isn't the only end of the horse that can speak. The tail can say quite a lot, actually. A tail may swish to simply remove flies. It may swish in combination with a wrinkled nostril or toss of the head, indicating mild annoyance. Or maybe it swishes vigorously and the hind leg comes up off the ground, either waving or stomping to warn that a kick may be on its way. A wringing, tense tail means that a horse is getting pretty tweaked, and an explosion may be on the way. A tail held high, perhaps arching up over the back, is most often seen in a playful or excited horse. When horses get spring fever or pretend to be afraid of nothing, part of that display is the high, arching tail coupled with rough snorts as they frolic and prance. One common trick some horses have is the ability to swish their tails aiming so the skirt whips you directly in the face, and usually in the eyes—tricky buggers!

Hind legs have their own ways to tell you things. That small lifting up and down, perhaps kicking at the ground are signs that a horse is either uncomfortable or anxious about something. Noticing this action can warn you to stay out of the way while also trying to determine the cause.

Of course, front or hind legs can often be stomped just to remove flies. Front legs can strike out and forward, either at another horse or from impatience. Along the same lines, heads can be tossed to scatter face flies, or just out of boredom. Learning to distinguish your horse's body language is not only a useful way to discover what may be upsetting him, it's also a good tool for staying safe.

FLIGHT OR FIGHT

This is a term that you may be familiar with. Prey animals, those that others hunt for food, are flight animals, meaning their instinct is to avoid danger by running away. Predators, animals that eat, or prey on others tend to fight off danger. Any animal pushed to its limits will reverse roles if it's in their best interest for survival.

Horses are flight animals. They may bicker among themselves, but when danger appears, they run. However, a horse who feels threatened and sees no escape route will turn and fight. They have some powerful tools at their disposal for either reaction. In flight, their ability to stand and run within hours of being born is one asset. Their keen hearing, sense of smell, and ability to see almost all around them gives them the advantage of detecting threats early. Those long, powerful legs and huge lungs give them the power and speed to get away far and fast.

When cornered, a horse will often rear and strike with a front leg; a blow from rock-hard hoof with the power of 1,000 pounds behind it can easily break bones. They may lunge and bite—those powerful jaws can deliver a grip of 500 pounds per square inch (psi). When the jaws close, they have to reach a certain point in order to open again, creating a distinct disadvantage for any enemy caught and fighting for release. For comparison, a human jaw has a bite strength of 200 psi, and a Rottweiler, the dog with the most powerful bite strength, is only 328 psi. The kick from the hind leg of a horse, which can be aimed, low, high, straight back, or even sideways, can pack a blow that measures over 2,000 pounds of direct force (psi)!

So, while they are clearly not defenseless, they are still flight animals. We must keep this in mind whenever we are around them. They have very quick reflexes, and even the quietest horse can react if startled. By tilting and either lowering or raising their heads they have almost 360 degree vision. Yet they do have blind spots, particularly when at rest and standing straight. Directly in front and directly behind are the two best known blind areas for a horse, especially if the person or object is close. On top of the back and under the belly are others that people often forget about. Touching a horse suddenly under the belly can earn you a swift, painful knock from a hind foot.

Since running away is one of their strengths, you want to keep a horse tied in a safe way, using a quick-release type of knot. There is equipment you can buy that will open, release, or intentionally break with enough pressure; though some horses learn this and will use it to fake being afraid in order to be free, it's better to be safe than sorry. Horses can easily break their halter, a lead rope tying them to something, the thing they are tied to, or, if it is a post, even pull it from the ground. This creates a bigger issue, as the horse now has a very scary object chasing them.

OVERALL APPEARANCE

Taking a good look at your horse every day can allow you to pick up on issues quickly, such as illness or injury. It can let you know if your horse, to put it bluntly, is happy or not. A sick or injured horse will often stand away from others with its head lowered. Its eyes might be dull. Or it may be rolling and kicking and nipping at its sides—sure signs of a colic, or stomachache. You might notice your horse being a little lethargic, or not cleaning up its food. All of these are signs of something amiss that your horse depends on you to fix.

Horses are big, beautiful, strong, and can be dangerous. Learning to read your horse's mood can help you predict his behavior, anticipate a reaction, and teach you what your horse will tolerate and what he doesn't particularly care for. Most of all, by understanding what your horse is saying, you can learn his mood and monitor his health with fairly good accuracy.

STORY: THE MOST FAMOUS HORSE IN THE MOVIES

Trigger, the golden Palomino stallion ridden by actor and cowboy Roy Rogers, was a well-known hero of the screen. His original name was Golden Cloud, and for Rogers, it was love at first sight. Golden Cloud was one of several horses brought in to audition for a role in the movie titled *Under Western Stars*, and after their first ride, no other horses were even considered.

Rogers bought Golden Cloud for $2,500 to ensure the two of them could continue to make movies together. He was referred to as the smartest horse in movies, and could perform more than 100 tricks. An actor friend, Smiley Burnett, once said, "As quick as that horse of yours is, you ought to call him Trigger." The nickname rang true, so the golden horse was forever after called Trigger.

Trigger was known to be a gentle, well-mannered, and patient horse. He would stand quietly for hours being admired by fans. Trigger starred in more than 88 movies and made appearances in over 100 TV shows, and was even briefly featured as the star of his own comic book.

Trigger lived out his years at Rogers' ranch, and died in 1965 at age 30.

9

INJURIES AND ILLNESS

" *Yet when books have been read and reread, it boils down to the horse, his human companion, and what goes on between them.*

—WALTER FARLEY

To go into much detail about the possible types of injuries and illnesses that horses are prone to is beyond our reach here. It is always better to live by the axiom, "When in doubt, call the vet."

However, there are things to watch for, actions to take, and care you can administer yourself, either in the case of something minor or as you wait for the vet to arrive. Teach yourself these three steps: notice, assess, treat. If you care for your horse daily, you will likely notice the first moment something is not right. Then, try to determine what kind of issue it is—a wound, illness, or lameness—and assess the severity. After that, decide how you will act—how you will treat the problem. In this case, treating the issue may be anything from cleaning up a small scrape to calling the veterinarian asap.

INJURIES - BRUISES, NICKS, CUTS, SCRAPES, AND WORSE

Horses are horses and often come in from the pasture with small wounds or have minor issues. It's good to have basic knowledge about how to assess the severity of injuries, and to be able to treat them, if possible.

Bruises

For things like bruising, this is most often associated with the sole of the hoof. A bad step on a rock, or too much work on a hard surface like a road can create bruising. When the sole is washed off, you may even be able to detect a discoloration or dent. Typically, the horse will just act slightly tender when moving. If the farrier pares away some of the sole, you can often see the bruise clearly. Time and discontinuing the activity are the best cure. If your horse has particularly tender feet that bruise easily, shoes with or without protective pads might be in order.

For body bruises, often the only way to detect them is to notice your horse is sensitive in a certain area while being groomed. A kick or bite from a pasture mate, a hard knock on a log or jump rail, or a fall can cause bruised, sore areas on your horse. If there is swelling, applying an ice pack or hosing with cold water a few times a day for the first two to three days can help. If the horse isn't too bothered, then as long as his saddle or other equipment won't irritate the area, he's probably fine to ride.

Minor Cuts and Scrapes

Small cuts, nicks, and scrapes or abrasions are commonplace with horses. Over time, you will learn to recognize what is or is not a big deal. There are basic steps to take to care for such minor wounds:

- If a wound is fresh and still bleeding, place a clean piece of gauze or towel over it and apply steady pressure with your hand for several minutes. When you remove your hand, the bleeding should be stopped or slowed considerably (if not, see next section).

- Clean the area gently but thoroughly using a disinfecting soap if on hand. Use more water than scrubbing. Rinse and pat dry.
- Add a very thin layer of an antibiotic ointment to help keep the area clean, and prevent dirt and flies from getting to it. It will also allow the skin to stay moist, which promotes healing.

  ○ It doesn't help to glob lots of ointment on a wound; in fact, it can hurt. Oxygen is important for healing, and a thick layer of goo will prevent air from getting to the area. It can also collect and trap dirt, which is exactly the opposite effect than you want.

- Once a scab is formed, you can leave it alone. Don't pick the scab! It will fall off when it is ready, and you will see healed skin and new hair growth underneath.
- Longer but shallow surface cuts can be treated the same way as long as they are not in a place where the skin will flex a lot (pulling the cut open again and again).
- Cuts on and around the legs can be wrapped to keep them clean. Remember to change the bandages.

Deep Cuts and Punctures

It is sometimes hard to tell how deep a wound is from the outside. You will need to call your veterinarian: if a wound is bleeding profusely—even after applying pressure (see above); if the wound is large and open; or if there seems to be a hole or puncture wound. They can properly clean the wound, then check for any foreign bodies—such as a splinter or nail—and remove them. The vet can also determine if the horse will need stitches to keep the wound closed while healing.

They can also administer antibiotics, and, if necessary, give your horse an anti-tetanus shot. These types of wounds heal slowly, so be patient and keep your horse's activity to a minimum until the vet removes the stitches or says he is healed.

Lameness, or, Why Is He Walking That Way?

Horses rely on their feet and legs for everything. When an injury occurs or an infection goes too deep, your horse will let you know by limping, shortening his gait, or refusing to bear much weight on a leg. Determining precisely where the injury is and what is causing it is another opportunity for you to learn from your vet. Some diseases can cause lameness, as can the natural aging process or hard work due to arthritis or inflammation.

There are hundreds of causes for lameness, whether it's minor tenderness or major limping, temporary events, such as a stone in the foot or a *splint* acting up, or major issues, like fractures or pulled tendons and ligaments.

COMMON HEALTH ISSUES

There is, unfortunately, an ever-growing list of diseases that can affect our horses. You will decide on which ones to vaccinate your horse against in consultation with your vet. Where you live, what types of environments your horse is exposed to, and how many horses are living with yours are all things to consider. At a minimum, you will give your horse an annual *rabies* vaccine (just like your dog or cat), and one for *tetanus*, often called "lock-jaw;" both are fatal blood diseases which can infect your horse through wounds and bites.

Respiratory infections are common in horses. Some are potentially more serious than others, and vaccines for those are often required by barns, not because they are particularly deadly, but because they are considered highly transmissible, meaning they can pass quickly through the air from horse to horse. There are also viruses that horses can get from tainted water, grass, hay, or from contact with sick horses or the spaces they have been in.

In the US, any horses being sold or transported are required to get a test every year for equine infectious anemia (EIA), an often fatal and incredibly transmissible disease. The test is more commonly known by the name Coggins Test, after Dr. Leroy Coggins, the vet who formulated it. Even if your horse lives alone and never leaves your property, do other horses come and go? Do your neighbors have horses? A mosquito or horse fly that bites an infected horse can then travel over a mile and bite another horse, thereby transferring the disease. Part of good horsemanship is not only protecting your own horse, but thinking about others, as well.

Detecting Disease

Follow the same protocol as above—notice, assess, treat—when it comes to days your horse is not feeling his best. Though the majority of equine illnesses tend to have detectable symptoms, not all of them do. For instance, if your horse is bitten by a tick carrying Lyme Disease, you may not know anything is wrong for months. Or you could detect intermittent issues like a lameness that comes and goes. Others may also lie dormant for a while, making determining when and how they contracted something very difficult. By that time, many diseases have progressed to a point where they are either very expensive or impossible to treat.

Noticing your horse's behavior every day is your first and best line of defense. Is he lethargic, does he have a runny nose or eyes? How about diarrhea, or perhaps a persistent cough? Now assess: Take your horse's vital signs; if there is no high fever, and both respiration and heart rates are near normal, isolate your friend from others and have the vet out as soon as you can. They will need to run tests and perform an exam to determine the cause of the symptoms.

If the body temperature, pulse or heart rate, and his respiration or breathing rate (TPR) of your horse is normal, and he seems to have an intermittent cough and a clear or slightly milky runny nose, then your horse may just have a cold. Like any other cold, it will probably pass. Deep persistent coughing, shortness of breath, and general difficulty breathing with or without hives appearing on the skin can indicate an allergic reaction, or a more serious respiratory issue, such as heaves—difficulty exhaling. Your vet can determine the cause and work with you to create a treatment or management plan as necessary.

Did You Know?

One of the best ways to monitor your horse for signs of illness or distress is to check his TPR. An average horse's temperature ranges from 99–100.5 degrees Fahrenheit, though a temperature of 98.5 up to 101 is not cause for alarm. The temperature is taken rectally, with a thermometer designed for horses. Wet or lubricate the tip, then gently insert it straight into the rectum until it is at least 2/3 of the way in. Wait a few minutes for an alcohol thermometer, or for the beep if using a digital one.

The average pulse rate is 32–38 beats per minute (bpm), but can range from 28–48 bpm. You can use a stethoscope to do this, but it is trickier than it looks. It is often much easier to find a vein near the surface of the skin, such as just inside the lower portion of the cheek, or inside the pastern area. Count how many beats you feel in 15 seconds, then multiply that number by four to get the bpm.

The average rate of respiration is 10–16 breaths per minute, but can range from 8–24. This can be done by patiently watching the horse's rib cage rise and fall, or by placing your palm in front of his nostrils and counting the breaths you feel. You can use the 15 seconds times four method above.

Learning how to measure these three elements is an important step in becoming a good horseman. If your horse seems off, maybe listless and with a runny nose, you will call your veterinarian. The first question they might ask is, "Do you know his vital signs?"

Tummy Troubles

Let's briefly review the most common digestive issues a horse can have, so that you know what to look for.

Choke

Choke is exactly what it sounds like. A mass of under-chewed food, usually grain, or a large piece of food, like a whole apple, gets stuck in your horse's esophagus. Often these masses slowly work their way down. The vet can give the horse a bit of mild sedative to relax the muscles, hoping the mass will then move on its own. Or, you can aid its passage with a little esophageal massage—gently massaging the mass with your hand on the outside of the neck to break up the clump or help it proceed to the stomach. Sometimes, a choke is harder to resolve, and when that happens the risks for scarring or a tear in the esophagus becomes a concern.

Prevention of Choke

There are some simple ways to help prevent choke from happening. If your horse tends to gobble his grain very quickly, place a large, clean stone or two in his feed dish. By having to move the stones around to get at the feed, he will eat smaller portions more slowly.

When feeding treats that are large enough to not be easily chewable, such as apples or carrots, cut them into pieces before giving them to your horse. If your pastures or hay are very dry, make sure there is always plenty of clean water for him to drink; even dry or clumped grass can cause a choke for some horses.

Colic

Colic is a very common, and often very serious ailment for a horse. The term itself simply means a bad stomach ache. But the causes and consequences for your horse are not so simple. The main causes of colic are gas, an intestinal spasm, a blockage or impaction in the bowel. Heavy loads of internal parasites and bad, moldy feed are other common causes.

When a horse is colicking, it will let you know by a combination of these behaviors:

- Rolling, getting up, and lying down repeatedly.
- Pawing, looking and/or kicking at the abdomen.
- Lack of sounds in the gut—a healthy horse's tummy always gurgles and groans.
- Not eating or drinking—not even if offered fresh grass or a treat.
- Listless demeanor, low head, and tail swishing.
- Producing no manure for several hours, but may pass gas.

If you suspect your horse may have colic, do not feed them. Keep them standing, even if you have to walk them for a long time to prevent them from lying down and rolling. If a horse rolls and has either gas, an obstruction, or an impaction, it is very easy for some part of their intestines to twist around on themselves, creating a *torsion*. Although a torsion can sometimes twist back with the help of your vet, it's not usual. A torsion is a serious, life-threatening issue that must be surgically corrected as quickly as possible.

Prevention of Colic

Good management is the best way to prevent colic. Some we have discussed already, such as feeding small meals more frequently, and making sure that the majority of the diet is fibrous, meaning hay or grass. Fiber keeps food moving and maintains the microbiome in the gut that helps with proper digestion.

Making sure your horse is drinking plenty of water will prevent dehydration; even mild dehydration can slow down his gut action and create an impaction—a mass of digested food that is too dry to move through the digestive tract. Sudden changes of weather can reduce a horse's urge to drink. That's why having a way to somewhat monitor his water intake can be so important.

Another culprit is too much grass, especially when your horse isn't used to it. As the grass ferments in his gut, it creates gas, and a gas colic is very painful. Of course, all food should be fresh; moldy grain and hay can cause colic, just as they would give you a tummy-ache. But here is one thing to note: horses can't vomit.

Whatever goes into a horse's stomach needs to pass through his system. Make sure that you take care of this most fragile system of the horse.

Diarrhea

While not a disease per se, but instead a symptom, diarrhea can be a serious worry for a horse. It is first and foremost a signal that something is wrong. There are many diseases and other causes of loose or runny manure, including viruses, infections, and internal parasites. Those should all be investigated, of course, but the immediate problem can be dehydration.

A lot of water passes through the more than 100 feet of tubes that make up a horse's digestive system from the stomach to the rectum. If a horse becomes dehydrated, from lack of water intake, or diarrhea, the process can be slowed considerably and can create a risk for colic. If allowed to become extremely dehydrated, it may require *intravenous* fluids to help the horse recover.

Ulcers

Did you know that horses can get ulcers? Stress, a poor diet, and internal infections can get ulcers started, and once they start, they can be hard to treat. For horses that work hard or travel a lot to show, giving your horse supplements that can keep his stomach at the right *pH level*—meaning not too much or too little digestive acid—can prevent or alleviate them.

For all that they are big, powerful animals, horses can be pretty fragile, and succumb to issues just as we can.

When it comes to things like vaccinating your horse for the most prevalent diseases in your area, ensuring his diet is complete, treating a wound before it gets infected, or even detecting a lameness early in order to prevent further damage, an ounce of prevention is worth a pound ($$$$) of cure.

STORY: OLD BILLY AND FRIENDS

On average, horses live to around 25 years old, with a range of 20–30 years. Remember that is a range; some of the horses I teach on are happy and healthy at 33 and 34 years old! Ponies and donkeys tend to live longer. In fact, many ponies are still working and active well into their thirties. So how old can horses get?

Old Billy is still the record holder and considered to be the oldest horse that has ever lived. Old Billy was born in Woolston, Lancastershire, England in 1760, and died at the amazing age of 62 on November 27, 1822. He was a working horse most of his life, a barge horse that helped move barges up and down the rivers.

Billy's life after death is almost as fascinating as the length of his life. It seems that Old Billy's remains were separated—at least the parts of his head certainly were. The skin is at the Cecil Higgins Art Gallery and is still on display, while his skull is currently on display at the Manchester Museum.

The oldest horse currently alive is also in England. Now living in Brentwood, Essex, England, 51-year-old Shayne is still prone to the occasional frolic in his pasture. According to a nearby equine veterinarian, 51 is definitely a very old age; however, horses live longer now because of advances in both veterinary medicine and improvements in the nutrition of their feed (2023, Remus Sanctuary).

10

GET READY TO RIDE!

> *No one can teach riding so well as a horse.*
>
> — C. S. LEWIS

All the time and care that we put into our horses is generally to achieve a goal beyond just having a healthy horse; we want to ride! There are many things that go into learning to and preparing for a ride, and we'll look at the most essential ones. We will need a good basic knowledge of the parts of the horse, and how horses think and react. Knowing how they see the world is useful, too. More basic safety rules will be added to the ones we have already discussed. Then we will investigate various types of equestrian sports, learn the parts of a saddle and bridle, as well as how to *tack up* your horse, and cover some basics to good riding. Time to saddle up!

PREPARING FOR A RIDE

You know the first few steps. You've learned how to properly care for your horse so that he is in overall good condition to ride. You know how to tie him safely and how to groom him. During grooming you've checked the condition of his feet and looked for any injuries or signs of lameness or illness, so you know he is good to go for a ride. The next few steps will include:

- Placing the saddle and bridle on the horse.
- Wearing correct (safe) gear for your ride.
- Going through the phases of a ride from warm-up to cool-down.
- Taking care of your horse and tack after a ride.

Grooming for Riding

Proper grooming happens before every ride, and it also happens again afterwards. Grooming before you ride is absolutely necessary, not only to check your horse all over, but also because grooming makes sure that no dirt, mud, or burrs are stuck in the hair underneath where the tack will sit; hidden debris can cause sores and rubs, and may make your horse uncomfortable enough to react badly. If your horse has a burr under the saddle, he will likely not appreciate you sitting on top of it, grinding it in! Dirt under the girth or the bridle can create open sores that will have to heal before using the tack again.

After a ride, if your horse has gotten sweaty, you will either want to hose or sponge off the sweat to remove the salts and any gunk that has accumulated on his coat or skin. Otherwise you will need to wait until he is completely dry, and give him a brisk curry and hard brushing. Picking his feet afterwards is a good habit, too; you can check for any stones or other objects that may be stuck in the hoof before they can do much damage.

A Super-Muddy Horse

Where I live, the mud in spring and fall is thick and sticky. To get your horse completely clean before a ride would mean giving him a full bath every time. That is not good for your horse's skin, and it is impractical in a few ways. Bathing takes time, and you would want your horse to be mostly dry before tacking him up. Also, in many places it is too cold to bathe at all for six months or more, much less every day!

So what to do with a mud-caked mount? There are a few corners you can cut before you ride. You can put a thin, nylon sheet on your horse when turned out in mud. It will be light enough to not interfere with his natural ability to fluff his coat to keep warm, but it will keep most of his body clean; the mud will be on the sheet, rather than on his back and belly. With the saddle area protected, you just need to make sure the girth area is as clean as you can get it, maybe using a damp towel to help. The same idea can work for his head to remove any mud that might end up under the bridle. Brush away what is dry, and wipe away any wet that you can.

After your ride, the mud should be pretty dry. Your plastic curry or a shedding blade can be a great tool to gently scrub dried mud so you can brush it away.

YOUR TACK

Tack is a word that means the equipment we use to ride a horse. It includes the saddle, bridle, girth, saddle pads, and any other gear we need. The process of putting the saddle and bridle on your horse is called "tacking up." Adjusting the tack to properly fit is important, as is placing it correctly on the horse. Most tack is made of leather for several important reasons: leather used for tack is generally soft and supple with no sharp edges. Leather, when properly cleaned and maintained, lasts a very long time, and; in an emergency, if your horse gets caught up in something, leather will break, letting your horse escape the situation. Some tack is made from nylon, neoprene, or other synthetics. These are easy to clean, can last a long time, and can be fun because they come in different colors. They are not easily breakable, however, which can create a hazard for both you and your horse.

Saddles

There are different types of saddles depending on the style of riding you do. Most are built in essentially the same way and have the same basic parts. English and Western riding are the most common styles. The tack may look very different, but at its core, it should be fitted to and placed on the horse in the same way.

Most saddles are built on a tree, a rigid core that looks like the basic shape of the saddle's seat. On top of the tree are layers of padding and leather. The front is called the pommel, the back is the cantle, and the middle is the seat. They all have a girth, which is the band that attaches to one side of the saddle, goes under the horse's belly behind the front legs, and attaches to the other side. Girths can be made of different materials, though leather for English saddles, and thick, soft rows of string for Western are the most common.

Saddles have stirrups to support the rider's leg and help them balance if necessary. Stirrup leathers are long leather straps that attach to the saddle behind the pommel and just below the front of the seat. The leathers hang from a stirrup bar under the saddle skirt, and the stirrup or stirrup iron—the foot part—hangs from the leather. Stirrups can be adjusted to fit different-sized riders.

Saddles come in different seat sizes, too. A child should ride in a smaller saddle, perhaps 14–15 inches, whereas a large adult may need an 18-inch seat. They also need to fit the horse correctly. When placed on the horse's back, just behind the withers and top of the shoulder blade, the saddle should fit these parameters:

- The gullet should be clear off the horse's back from front to back.
- There should be at least three fingers height of clearance between the pommel and the withers.
- The seat of the saddle should appear level in the center, neither tipping up in front (pommel high, cantle low) or the back (pommel low, cantle high).

- When attached, the girth should hang straight down about a hand's width behind the horse's elbow. Too close, and it will rub the elbow sore, too far back and the saddle will press the horse's loins, while likely perching on his withers. This position will also prevent the girth from being properly tightened, so the saddle may slip and cause a fall.

A chestnut pony with well-fitted English tack ready for a ride. The pony has four white socks and a blaze, too.

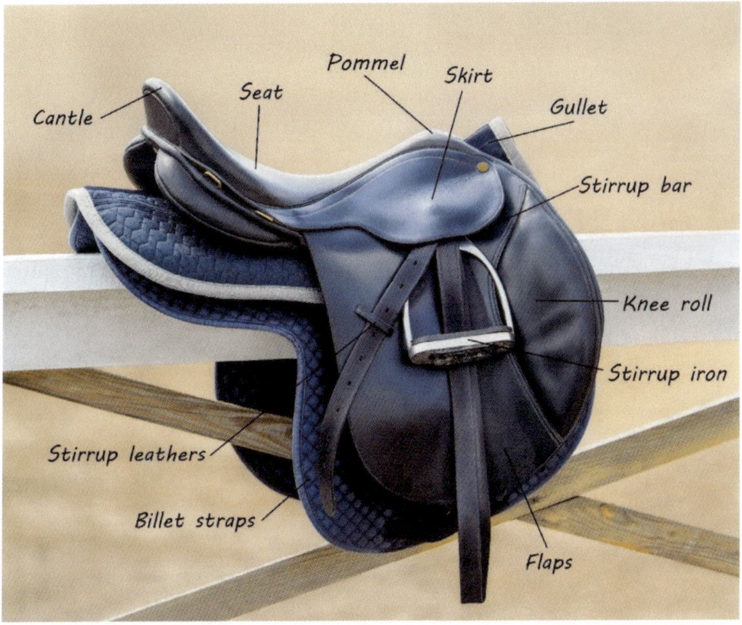
Pommel
Skirt
Seat
Cantle
Gullet
Stirrup bar
Knee roll
Stirrup iron
Stirrup leathers
Billet straps
Flaps

Western saddles have the same basic parts, with a few notable additions, such as fenders, latigos, swells, and maybe a horn. A girth for a Western saddle is called a cinch, and it is attached with a wide leather strap called a latigo that is tied around a D-shaped ring, or rigging, rather than to billet straps using buckles. Western saddles may also have two girths, with the second, or flank cinch, attached more toward the cantle of the saddle. This girth is not tight, rather it just helps stabilize the back half of the saddle.

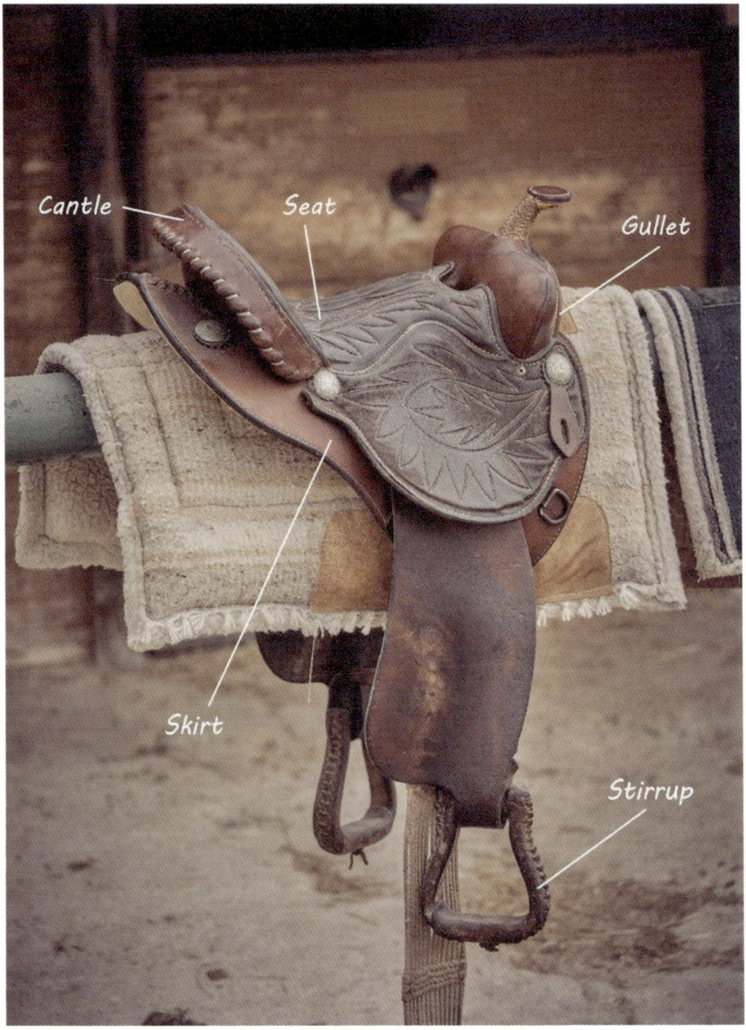
Cantle
Seat
Gullet
Skirt
Stirrup

A horse well-outfitted in Western tack.

Bridles

The bridle, the piece of equipment that goes on a horse's head that is used to offer the rider a way to communicate with their horse along with some control. A bridle may have a bit attached to it—that is the metal piece that goes in the horse's mouth and rests on the bars of the mouth between the front incisors and molars—but some do not. Bridles have reins that riders use to guide and steer.

English bridles tend to be used to steer a horse with direct reining, or using the left rein slightly back to go left, and the right rein slightly back to go right. The reins are attached directly to either side of the bit, and are joined together by a small buckle near the ends. They have a noseband, or cavesson, to help stabilize the horse's jaw and gently keep the mouth more closed to prevent the bit from sliding. English bridles also have a brow band that goes above the eyes and just below the ears to keep it securely on the horse's head. An English bridle without a bit is generally called a hackamore, with the reins attached on either side of the noseband.

Western bridles do not vary much from English ones. They may have a brow band, but often have one slot at the top that one ear goes through to hold the bridle in place, or may have two separate ear slots (described as single-eared or double-eared). Western bridles do not typically have a noseband or cavesson, but they may also be bitless, in which case they are a hackamore or sometimes a bosal. A bosal is a sturdy loop often made from rawhide leather. The reins attach to the bosal knot underneath the jaw. Western bridles most often have split reins, meaning that each rein is separate from the other. Since they are not attached, and can easily slide, they are longer than English reins, allowing them to drape down the opposite side and along the horse's shoulders.

Bits

There are so many kinds of bits! Some simple, some complicated, and some have flat chains or straps that run under the jaw. Essentially a bit is designed to create pressure that the horse is trained to respond to.

Bits can put pressure on several areas, including the bars of the mouth, the tongue, the palette or roof of the mouth, and the corners of the lips. Some bits have long sides that can exert pressure on the poll, or top of the head between the ears, and under the jaw with the strap or chain. Some are quite powerful and can cause pain and discomfort quickly, yet most are quite mild, exerting a gentler pressure.

One thing that all bits have in common is that, in the wrong hands, they can be abused. A rider's hands move and make mistakes, causing at the least confusion and mixed messages, and at the worst, damage to the horse through cruel and aggressive use. Be kind to your horse!

Auxiliary Tack

Just as there are many kinds of bits, there are many more pieces of tack and other equipment people might use on their horses for a variety of reasons. The most common, and most benign or harmless, are a martingale, breastplate, and crupper.

Martingales go around the horse's neck and attach at one end to the girth and at the other to the noseband. They should be adjusted so that the horse can raise and lower its head normally, but it will prevent the horse from flinging its head up and back. This behavior can make him difficult for the rider to control, and can put the rider at risk of getting their face badly smacked by the top of the horse's head. A running martingale is a variation that splits and attaches to each rein rather than to the noseband. It allows for greater freedom of movement for the horse, but if used incorrectly can put too much pressure on the mouth.

Breastplates have a strap that goes over a horse's withers, and attach to a broad band across his chest. That chest strap runs back and attaches to the girth on either side. Not a method of control, it prevents the saddle from sliding too far back on a horse, which is important when riding up and down hills.

A crupper is a sort of reverse breastplate. It is a strap that runs from the gullet of the saddle under the cantle, straight back to a padded loop around the dock of the horse's tail. This set-up prevents the saddle from slipping too far forward, a problem common in ponies with low withers.

CARING FOR YOUR TACK

Whether your tack is leather or nylon, taking good care of it will help it last a long time. Plus, by removing dirt and sweat regularly, you avoid making the tack brittle, which will prevent cracking and breaking. Dirt can also build up on the inner surfaces close to the horse's skin, which can create sores. Even the metal parts, like the buckles and stirrups, should be wiped down regularly. Bits should be rinsed and wiped clean after every ride.

Cleaning

Although synthetic materials, like nylon and neoprene, can be washed with soap and water, leather needs special care. Too much water will dry out the leather, but leaving tack dirty will make it crack and break. So dry is bad, and wet is bad. Each time you use your tack, or at least once a week, wipe everything down with a slightly damp rag. This will remove dust and grime. If there is sticky black gunk stuck to the leather, you can gently scrub it with an old toothbrush, then use the damp cloth afterward. Cleaners designed for leather can cause drying if used too often, so save those for really dirty tack or times when you will take everything apart for a good spring and fall treatment.

Using glycerine soap or another leather conditioning product for cleaning. Take a slightly damp sponge or clean rag, add some of the glycerine to the rag, and rub it in well to every surface using small, circular motions. If the leather is dry, you can use an oil to give it another coat in the same way. Let the leather sit for a few minutes, then buff it with a soft, dry cloth. Your tack is now clean!

Storage

All tack, even synthetics, can get moldy if not stored properly. Ideal conditions may be hard to find, but you want to keep everything in a place that offers most of these features:

- Moderate humidity—moist air creates mold, and dry air dries out leather quickly.
- Moderate temperature—extreme heat and cold can cause damage too, especially to synthetics which crack easily.
- Out of direct sunlight—sunlight can damage a variety of materials.

If you need to store your tack for an extended period of time, give it a thorough cleaning and oiling, and store it in a cloth bag. Put the cloth bag in a dry trunk, or wrap a plastic bag over the cloth.

TACKING UP YOUR HORSE

Here he is, your clean horse standing before you, ready to be tacked up. You could, of course, jump right to bridling if you want to ride bareback, but let's go through the whole process, starting with saddling.

Saddling

Start on the horse's left by placing the saddle pad on his back at the withers or a little forward. Gently place the saddle on his back so that the pad shows equally all the way around the saddle. Check to make sure there are no lumps or folds in the pad. Attach the pad to the saddle, if possible. Pull the pad up into the gullet, and slide the saddle and pad back a bit until the seat is level, and the front of the saddle rests just behind the top of the shoulders. By pulling back, rather than forward, you avoid bunching up the horse's hair, which may make him uncomfortable.

Moving to the off (right) side, attach the girth or cinch to the billets or rigging. Let it hang straight down, and move back to the near side, then, reaching under his belly, grab the girth and bring it over toward you. Attach the girth on this side, but make it just snug enough to keep the saddle in place for now. Many a kind horse has been turned into a grumpy biter from having their girth tightened too quickly! You can check and tighten it some after bridling, and once more before you get on.

Bridling

Bridling can be tricky to master at first. Some horses are reluctant to open their mouths for the bit, and some like to play the game of "see how high I can lift my head." Bridling can require several lessons on how to correctly fit one, and which straps attach where.

Once again standing on the near side of your horse, and not directly in front of him, place the reins over the neck. If he's tied, untie the lead and remove the halter, placing both out of harm's way. Holding the top, or crown piece, of the bridle in your right hand, either wrap your arm under his jaw or drape it over his head so that the bridle is hanging in front of the face.

Place the bit in your left palm, making sure the palm is flat so your fingers are out of reach, and while pulling gently upward on the crown with your right hand, bring the bit up to the horse's mouth, as if you are about to feed him a treat. Make sure the bit is heading to where the teeth join, and not up under his lips to his gums. At this point, most horses will open their mouths and you can pull the bridle up, getting the bit the rest of the way into the mouth.

Next, still holding the crown piece, push one ear forward and slip the bridle over it. Repeat with the other ear. Make sure the bridle sits correctly on the head and that the browband and cavesson are straight. Put the ends of the cavesson underneath the cheek pieces, then fasten the buckle under the jaw just tight enough to allow two of your fingers to slip underneath between the band and the jaw, or one finger at the top of his nose. Now secure the throatlatch, which conveniently goes around the horse's throatlatch; it should angle slightly so that it goes around the throat and not around the cheeks. Tighten the throatlatch until you can only place a flat fist between the horse's cheek and the strap. Looser, and it will serve no purpose; tighter and it could interfere with his breathing or comfort. The throatlatch is something you hope you will never need, but you will appreciate it a lot if you do. It's one job is to keep the bridle on the horse's head in case of some event that might catch the bridle and try to pull it forward—this includes you, should you end up flying over the horse's head in a fall. Hey, it happens.

WHAT WILL YOU WEAR?

You know how to get your horse dressed for a ride. What about you? There are lots of riding-specific clothes you can wear, and at their origins they all had a specific purpose. But if you are a casual trail rider, all you need are:

- Boots, low or tall, with a distinct heel to prevent your feet from slipping through the stirrups.
- Long pants to keep your legs protected. They could be jeans or riding breeches.
- Gloves to keep your hands from getting sore should your horse pull away quickly.
- A certified riding helmet to protect your brain and lessen the chance for a concussion in a fall.

The rest is up to you; now you are both ready to go!

Did You Know?

By knowing the weight of your horse you can determine how heavy a rider they can carry. Even though they look full-grown on the outside, a horse's skeleton is still growing and hardening until they are about four years old. It's best to wait to ride your horse until they are at least that age to prevent doing any damage. Once they are old enough, they should carry riders no bigger than 15–18% of their body weight.

This pair shows a well-turned-out rider with excellent position, and a beautifully groomed horse with beautiful hunter braids.

11

RIDING BASICS

> *We have almost forgotten how strange a thing it is that so huge and powerful and intelligent an animal as a horse should allow another, and far more feeble, animal to ride upon its back.*
>
> — PETER GRAY

There is no substitute for good riding instruction to help you learn, stay safe, and keep your horse going well. Reading and watching videos can help, but having a knowledgeable riding teacher train you is the only way to really improve. They can recognize what you need to fix, and tell you how. They can tell you when you are doing something just right, or can offer assistance on how to make it better. Most of all, they can see you. Watching someone else is not the same as being seen. Even if you could see yourself, you may not always know how to fix your mistakes properly.

MOUNTING AND DISMOUNTING

Getting on and off of your horse should be done confidently, quietly, and relatively quickly. Like most skills, it may take a bit of practice until you are smoothly swinging over his back, rather than scrambling on or kicking the horse in the butt. A tool you should definitely have is a mounting block. This can be any sturdy, stable object that allows you to get higher up so that you reduce the pull on your horse's back as you mount. It can be a specially-purchased item, a homemade set of one or two steps, or a convenient stump from a log. Reducing the sideways torque of the horse's spine is a great way to keep his back straight and strong. It also reduces the pull against your saddle, which over time can stretch things, or, if the girth is loose, make the whole saddle slip to the side.

Before you try to mount, make sure your girth is now tight enough and that your stirrups are hanging down.

Mounting

Bring your horse's left side up next to the mounting block. Stepping on the block, hold your reins in your left hand at the horse's withers. This will allow you to stop him should he try to walk forward. Do not hold the front of the saddle, as this will create even more pull to one side. Place your left foot in the stirrup with your toes pointing forward (so you don't poke him in the ribs as you mount). Place your right hand on the cantle. Take a few breaths, while gently bouncing on your right foot. Count to three, then push up with your right foot until you are straight up, balancing your weight on your left stirrup and your hands. Move your right hand forward while swinging your right leg over and across to the horse's right side. Gently sit down in the saddle; try not to drop hard into it. It's not nice for his back, and it may startle him. Place your right foot in the stirrups and take your reins in both hands. Voila! You are on and ready to ride.

Dismounting

Though it may seem silly, there are some better ways to get off a horse than others. Mounting and dismounting are sometimes referred to as the scariest six seconds in riding: three for mounting, three for dismounting. This is because in these few moments, you are neither firmly on the ground nor safely on the horse's back. You are somewhere in between, and that place is unbalanced and insecure.

Two safe ways to dismount are to vault or reverse the mount. Vaulting requires taking both of your feet out of the stirrups, then, in one swift motion, move your upper body forward to the right, and swing your right leg back over his rump to the left. Then, essentially, let your body drop so you land on your feet. Remember to continue holding the reins. You don't want a nice ride spoiled by a loose horse.

Reversing the mount means taking only your right foot out of the stirrup. Then, standing up on your left stirrup, swing the right leg over the rump. Your hands should be in the same position they were for mounting, with the left holding the reins at the withers, and the right on the cantle of the saddle. Pause there, and remove your left foot from the stirrup. From here, you can jump down, or if necessary, lower yourself slowly to the ground on both feet.

Dismounting while keeping the left foot in the stirrup and putting the right foot all the way to the ground is an easy way to fall over, or get caught in the stirrup if your horse moves at that moment. Swing a leg forward over the neck is problematic, too. A horse can quickly raise its head very high. You might kick your friend in the neck, or, if your leg is almost over, get suddenly helped quickly to the ground. This technique also means that you cannot keep the reins in your hand at all times, giving your horse another moment to choose to wander off.

HOW TO SIT ON A HORSE

When sitting on a horse, you want to achieve 3-way balance, meaning back to front, left to right, and top to bottom. You want to rest squarely on both seat bones, sitting up tall with shoulders relaxed. Allow your legs to hang against the horse. There is no need to grip hard, just use enough strength to maintain your position. If looking at a rider from the side, you should be able to draw an imaginary line from the rider's ear, through the shoulder, then the hip, and ending just in front of the heel. This "ear-shoulder-hip-heel" alignment will keep you in good balance while allowing for freedom of movement on the horse.

The rider's heel should be below the level of the stirrup iron when the foot is in the stirrup. To measure the correct length, sit with your legs dangling out of the stirrups. Gently bang your legs against the stirrup iron. Adjust the stirrup leather so that ideally it will hit at or just below your ankle bone, maybe a bit higher if you will be galloping and jumping. Make sure the stirrups are even when compared to each other.

Carry the reins, whether in one hand or two, in a gently closed fist with your thumb on top to help prevent them from slipping and getting too long. Your elbow should be bent but relaxed, and your arm should create a straight line from your elbow through the reins to the bit.

While riding we communicate with the horse by using aids. Aids can be verbal or physical. When you are ready to move off, you can do this verbally, with a cluck or saying "walk on," or with aids, by briefly and gently closing your inner calf against the horse's sides. If he does not respond, you can ask again, with a stronger squeeze perhaps combined with a cluck or verbal cue.

Learning to ride in balance at a walk is not too hard, though most people ride with grip, rather than balance. Riding at a faster pace, like a trot or a canter takes more practice to do well. When riding, you want to keep your balance in order for the horse to better keep his own, rather than compensating for you all the time. Learning to move with a horse, allowing his body motion to go through you rather than resisting it, is important to master at all the different gaits. Let's look at the gaits now.

Gaits of a Horse

Horses can walk, trot, canter, gallop, and run. Some breeds have gaits that are specific to them, either through breeding or traditional training, but we will focus on the main three: walk, trot, and canter. Every horse has its own natural tempo, or speed, to its walk, trot, and canter, but each gait has the same rhythm, or pattern of footfalls, for all horses.

The Walk

A walk is a four-beat, lateral gait. A lateral gait means that the horse moves the legs on one side, then the legs on the other side, creating a left-left, right-right movement. This is why the walk feels like a sashay, a long gait with a rolling swing. The walk is also the most stable gait, with three hooves being on the ground at a time. It is also the same whether the horse is traveling to the right (clockwise) or to the left (counterclockwise).

One full stride (or complete step, meaning all four feet have progressed) of a walk works as follows: Starting with the left hind, as it steps forward, the left front moves to allow space for the hind leg to land. After that, the right hind swings forward, stepping into or near the hoofprint created by the right front. Now we can better describe the sequence of footfalls for a walk: left hind-left front, right hind-right front. An average horse travels about 4–6 miles per hour (mph) when walking.

The Trot

The trot is a two-beat, diagonal gait. Every two beats equals one stride. The horse's left hind and right front move together as a pair, then the right hind and left front together. The horse essentially bounces from one pair to the other, an action that creates a motion similar to when humans jog, bouncing from one foot to the other. Trotting can be fast or slow, and smooth in some horses but quite bumpy in others. It is the most often used gait for horses both when ridden and when free. Trotting is about twice as fast as a walk, and less tiring than a canter or gallop; a trot can be maintained for relatively long periods of time. A horse moves on average 8–12 mph in a trot. Like the walk, the trot is also a steady, balanced gait, with two feet on the ground at a time, and is the same when traveling in either direction.

One way to make a trot easier to ride is to *post*, or move up and down in the saddle matching the horse's rhythm. If the trot is a one-two, one-two steady rhythm, then the rider can basically stand-sit, stand-sit which prevents the rider from getting bounced all around, and saves the horse from having a rider pounding on its back. A common myth is that only

English riders post the trot, but not Western riders. A good Western rider knows how and when to post to a trot, in order to both bounce less and save the back of the horse.

The Canter

Horses have four legs, so a four-beat walk and a two-beat trot make sense: one leg at a time makes four beats, and two at a time makes two beats. The canter is a three-beat gait, so two legs move independently, and two as a pair. The canter rolls from back to front and diagonally through the horse. Learning to sit relaxed and in balance in a canter takes some practice precisely because of this rolling action and because it changes if the horse is moving clockwise or counter-clockwise. When cantering, the rider should endeavor to sit quietly, allowing the horse to move the rider with the motion. One common way to explain to a rider how to sit a canter is to have them "sit on their back pockets."

A canter starts with a single hind leg. When moving to the right, the left hind initiates to stride, followed by the pair of right hind-left front, and last the right front. Weirdly, this last step by the front leg is called the leading leg, or, simply, the lead. When a horse moves clockwise, the right front should be the leading leg; when moving counter-clockwise, it should be the left front. The rhythm is three beats, followed by a small pause, when all four feet are off the ground. This is called a moment of suspension. For some horses, the moment of suspension is very brief, but for others it is almost a full fourth beat long. A canter stride covers a lot of ground, with an average speed of 12–15 mph.

STORY: TWO BOYS AND A PONY

In the summer of 1967, two brothers from Massachusetts set off in a cart pulled by their trusted Shetland pony, King. They were bound for Montreal, Canada to see the World's Fair. It took them almost a month to cover the 330 miles. Tony, the older brother, would often get out of the cart and help King push it up hills while Jeff steered the cart.

At first, the boys had friend's homes to stay in for the night, but the farther they went, the fewer plans they had. Stopping at homes that had fencing and animals, they asked strangers for shelter and food for the three of them. Soon, their journey had become big news, and people began walking with them through towns, stopping to see them along the way, and offering them food and beds for the night—and, of course, for King, too.

The journey went from Massachusetts through New Hampshire and Vermont, and up to the border. After a slight delay crossing into Canada, they arrived at the fair the following day. The delay was caused by the Border Patrol officers not wanting them to come in until the boys knew where they would be staying that night. After several days of being treated like VIPs at the fair, boys, pony, and cart all arrived safely home, only this time it took only a few hours in a truck!

12

HORSE SPORTS AND ACTIVITIES

" *A canter is a cure for every evil.*

— BENJAMIN DISRAELI

Time for some fun! There are so many sports we can participate in with our horses, and many ways to enjoy riding and spending time with them. While all riding is considered a sport, especially by those who ride, some require more strength and skill than others. Equine activities can include shows and competitions, for sure, but the list also includes trail riding and other non-competitive ways to participate.

Let's explore ten broad categories of equestrian activities and look at a brief overview of each. Again, with so many choices, this isn't going to be a complete list, so if your favorite doesn't show up here, that isn't a sign that it's less fun or popular. On the other hand, you might see some activities you'd never heard of, and may want to try them at some point in your riding career.

RACING

The three main types of racing are flat racing, harness racing, and steeplechase.

Flat Racing

Flat racing generally occurs on a track of some kind, and is what Thoroughbreds and Quarter horses (and sometimes Arabians) do. It can also include long-distance races, such as the one featured in the movie *Hidalgo*. The Kentucky Derby is an example of a famous flat race. A line of horses stand in a set of gates. When the bell rings, the gates are opened and the horses all leap out, or break, and begin running. Distances vary, but one of the longest, most well-known races is the Belmont Stakes in New York, the third leg of the Triple Crown. The Belmont is one-and-a-half miles long. The longest flat race in the world is the Queen Victoria Stakes in Great Britain, at a distance of two miles. An average speed for a Thoroughbred in a flat race is 30–35 mph. Quarter horses can reach higher speeds but for shorter distances. In a 1/4-mile long race, a Quarter horse can reach speeds of 45–50 mph.

Thoroughbred horses in a flat race.

Harness Racing

Harness racing is a speed sport for Standardbred horses. The horses are hitched to a small two-wheeled cart called a sulky in which the jockey sits. Harness races are typically a mile long and run at speeds of about 30 mph.

There are two types of harness racers: trotters have huge, fast, ground-covering trots; and pacers, whose gait is bred in. Pacers run in a lateral two-beat motion, with both front and hind legs on one side moving together, then the legs on the other side go. It is a very fast gait, and pacer is generally faster than a trotter.

Steeplechase or Jump Racing

A steeplechase or jump race is a Thoroughbred race that combines speed and power. Steeplechasing started in Ireland in the 1700s as a cross-country race from one church steeple to the next—that's where the name comes from. Hurdle races are run in laps on a course of about 2–3 miles long over jumps about four ft high; at least one-third of the height is brush along the top. The horses jump over the solid, lower portion, and allow their legs to pass through the brush layer. Timber races are generally 3–4 miles long, with solid fences ranging from 3 ft 6 in. up to 5 ft in height. There may be 20 or more obstacles in a jump race.

RODEOS

There are many events that happen at a rodeo, which is a type of competition that bases results on judging, time, and scores. Rodeo classes can include barrel racing, team penning and team roping, sorting, and steer wrestling. Bull and bronco riding are also rodeo sports.

Trail classes

These classes may be part of a rodeo, a larger horse show, or just held as competitions by themselves. In a trail class, horses and riders must complete a course of obstacles, which may include bridges, ramps, seesaws, patterns ridden in reverse, weaving, and opening and closing gates, plus many more. These classes test the skill and trust between the partners. In a trail class, your horse may even have to cope with you picking up a rubber chicken and putting it safely in a mailbox! Each activity in the class is given a score, then the totals are averaged.

Gymkhanas

Gymkhana is a sport consisting of a set of games. Though they are often associated with Western riding, English riders play gymkhana games, too. There are prizes for each game, as well as overall championships at a competition. Games can be almost anything from relays to pair-riding tests. There are elimination games, such as egg-in-spoon (don't drop the egg while riding), sit-a-buck (while riding bareback you must keep a dollar bill under your leg), and musical stalls. There are trail obstacle challenges, and speed games like pole-bending. Use your imagination to create your own and host a games day!

TEAM SPORTS

Horses and riders in teams play in a variety of games. The most well-known is polo, which is kind of like mounted field hockey, in which each rider uses a long mallet to get a ball down the field and into the opponent's goal. Polo was started in Persia, and is the oldest team sport in the world

Polocrosse, a lacrosse and polo hybrid, is played pretty much like regular lacrosse, except on horseback. Riders may use only the basket of their stick to move the ball down the field of play.

Horseball does not require a mallet or lacrosse stick. The game uses a ball about the size of a soccer ball, but this one is covered in handles or grab straps. Riders may only use their hands to keep the ball in play; if it is dropped, a rider must be skillful enough to reach down and grab one of the handles as they race by.

EVENTING

This is a popular sport that combines a discipline and communication test in dressage, an endurance test in cross country jumping, and a speed and fitness test in show-jumping. A three-day event breaks each portion up over the course of the day, with typically longer cross-country rounds, and more challenging jumping courses. A three-phase is usually a one-day event that covers all three sports in a shorter, generally easier format. The three stages can be briefly described as follows:

- **Dressage**—An equestrian discipline that requires highly skilled movements be performed by horse and rider in a predetermined pattern. It is a graceful sport that requires great strength from the horse and years of training. It is like a compulsory movements skating program. It is usually the first event, to prove that very fit horses can remain quiet and disciplined enough to dance with their rider.
- **Cross-country**—A course of jumps over uneven terrain (meaning not on a smooth, flat track). Cross-country jumps are solid, and do not break. They may be made of timber, stone walls, or gates and fencelines. The sport also includes water jumps—where the horse must jump into water, navigate an obstacle, and jump out—as well as banks, drops, and ditches.

It is a test of strength and overall fitness and stamina.

- **Stadium jumping**—Generally saved for the last phase, it can show that even after an exacting dressage test and grueling cross-country course, the horse is fit and agile enough to jump fences and navigate a course of easy-to-knock down rails within a time limit.

HORSE SHOWS

A horse show is any gathering of horses and riders in which competitors enter different classes depending on their ability or sport, and are judged as a group by an expert in that activity. Horse shows can be fun, low-key local events for amateurs and children, or they can be as famous and fancy as the Olympics!

Many different disciplines, or styles of riding, are seen at horse shows, and frequently more than one at a single event such as:

- **Western**—including western pleasure, reining patterns, and western equitation.
- **English**—including hunters, jumpers, dressage, and pleasure.

- **Saddleseat**—specifically for certain breeds, such as Morgans, Saddlebreds, Arabians, and gaited horses.

A gray Welsh pony and their rider in good form over a jump at a local horse show.

AND SO MUCH MORE

It can't be said too often how many different ways there are to enjoy your horse. Let's wrap up this section by listing just a few more.

Trail Riding

Whether it's a casual ride with friends in the woods, a long-distance ride, endurance rides, or horse camping, these are all ways to get out of the riding ring and into nature with your equine friend. Please note that, like swimming, no one should ride away from home alone. Find a buddy, or at the very least give someone your route and estimated time of return.

Two riders on a "hack," or ride outside of a ring.

Driving

Driving can be a really fun way to be with your horse, but not on his back. It can be as simple as a pony pulling a small cart around the yard and dirt roads, it can be for work like pulling logs, or it can be very challenging, as in combined driving—a sport that includes driven dressage, cross-country, and a tight obstacle course called hazards instead of jumping. It may also make you think of the Clydesdales or Percherons, among other draft breeds, that pull the big wagons with a team of 2–8 horses, or perhaps the fancy carriages pulled by one or two horses that we see in old movies.

Foxhunting

Believe it or not, this sport is alive and well across a lot of the world. Though it originated with the use of dogs for hunting and the horses just a means to keep up, it has evolved over time. These days most hunts are what are termed "drag hunts," meaning they lay a scent for the hounds to follow, rather than search for wild quarry. It combines the skill and thrill of riding cross-country with an appreciation of the hounds and how they work as a team. It is also an opportunity to ride on land otherwise unavailable to many of us due to where we live. In return, foxhunters respect the landowners, often helping maintain the property, and try to preserve land and take good care of it.

CLUBS AND GROUPS

Nearby you might be surprised to find some groups of like-minded horse lovers. Joining these groups is a way to make friends who share your passion and to keep learning more about horses. For many, you don't need to own a horse of your own, or to have a truck and trailer to get your horse around.

A lot of local barns offer camps and clubs for riders who do not have their own horses. The riders use the schoolhorses that belong to the farm for lessons, trail rides, and other learning experiences. They might take field trips to other horse facilities to see what it's like at, say, a racing stable or an equine veterinary clinic.

Pony Club is an organization originally started in England that spread to other countries over time. The Pony Club system often requires members to have their own horses, but not always. A barn hosting a pony club may allow members to lease a schoolhorse for club activities. Pony Club is a very knowledge-focused, hands-on organization. Members progress through various levels of proficiency in riding, horse health, and stable management. There may be more than one correct way to do things with a horse, but with Pony Club you will never learn the wrong way.

4-H clubs often have a special focus, such as sewing, outdoor adventures, woodworking, or cows. Learning about horses is one of those focuses for clubs across the US and even some in Canada. Members do not usually need to have their own horses as riding is not the primary focus; learning all about horses is. 4-H offers the opportunity for working on horse-related projects and to learn breeds, play games that teach colors, parts of the horse, saddle, bridle, and more. There are presentations you can give on a topic of your choice, and even quiz-style competitions based on your knowledge of horses and their conformation, or the way they are built.

For older riders, there are organizations across the US that provide a way for middle school, high school, and college students to compete even if they do not have a horse. These teams compete against other schools of the same grades, and earn points both as individuals and for their teams.

The American Equestrian League (AEL), and the Interscholastic Equestrian Association (IEA) offer opportunities for middle and high-schoolers in hunt seat equitation both on the flat (or walk, trot, and canter) and over fences. The Interscholastic Dressage Association (IDA) hosts teams made of riders from some high schools as well as colleges. They ride strictly in dressage and consist of teams of four riders, though a school can have more than one IDA team.

The largest of these organizations is the Intercollegiate Horse Shows Association (IHSA). With zones all across the country, IHSA include both Western reining and equitation and English hunt seat riding opportunities. It is open to any college that wishes to join, and each member college hosts or helps host competitions throughout the season, which runs from early fall to the end of May, when the National Finals are held. The levels of riding range from walk/trot only for relative beginners through to the Open levels, which include the ability to jump fences of 3 ft 3 in. or to ride increasingly difficult reining patterns at speed.

GOT A MINUTE?

The more you learn about horses, the more fulfilling you'll find spending time with them – and the better care you'll be able to take of them. And now you have a chance to spread that love to horses far and wide.

Simply by sharing your honest opinion of this book on Amazon, you'll show other young riders where they can find this essential knowledge… and that means a better life for more horses!

Thank you so much for your support. I'm so excited for your journey as a rider!

Scan the QR code for a quick review!

CONCLUSION

Do you know more about horses now than when you started this book? If so, mission accomplished. In particular, I hope you learned a fact or two that surprised you, read a story that you'd never heard of, and discovered a horse sport or activity that you can't wait to try.

Going back to the beginning of the horse's origins can give us a different perspective on how long these beautiful creatures have been around. Though we still don't know why they evolved to have temperaments that are, more or less, accepting of your partnership, we are certainly grateful.

Learning about how horses grow, and the correct terminology, or words, to describe them at different stages of development can help us understand them better, and to explain in part their behavior. While there are so many things to learn about parts of the horse, the tack, and the things we need to properly care for them, we now have a solid foundation, as well as a list of ways to remain safe around such powerful and skittish creatures.

While by no means a substitute for hands-on education with an experienced horse person, this book should allow you to speak knowledgeably about horses. Knowing how to describe a horse and how to watch for things like lameness or illness are important not just for those who own horses but for anyone planning to spend time around them.

There is so much more to learn and to know about horses and their care, and that includes all of the tack and equipment we didn't review, plus technique we need to truly learn to ride well. All that information could (and does) fill hundreds of books. This is just a start. You will learn much more along the journey from friends, professionals, and most of all, your horse.

APPENDIX I

A LIST OF POPULAR HORSE BREEDS AND THEIR AVERAGE WEIGHT AND SIZE (LEE, 2022)

Breed	Average Weight	Average Height
Andalusian	1200 – 1300 lbs	15–16 hands
Arabian	900 – 1200 lbs	14.1–15.1 hands
Appaloosa	1000 – 1300 lbs	14–15.2 hands
Belgian	1800 – 2200 lbs	15–16.3 hands
Clydesdale	1600 – 1800 lbs	15.3–17.1 hands
Dutch Warmblood	1200 – 1300 lbs	15.3–16.3 hands
Hanoverian	1200 – 1400 lbs	16–17.1 hands
Morgan	900 – 1200 lbs	14–15.1 hands
Percheron	1800 – 2100 lbs	15.1–17 hands
Quarter Horse	1000 – 1300 lbs	14–16.2 hands
Saddlebred	1000 – 1200 lbs	14.3–16.1 hands
Shire	1700 – 2700 lbs	16–17.3 hands
Mustang	800 – 1000 lbs	13–15 hands
Standardbred	1200 lbs	14.3–15.3 hands
Tennessee Walking Horse	900 – 1400 lbs	14.3–16 hands
Thoroughbred	1000 – 1300 lbs	15.2–17 hands
Welsh Pony (and Cob)	1000 – 1300 lbs	12–13.1 (13–14.1) hands
Shetland Pony	300 – 600 lbs	8.3–10.2 hands

APPENDIX II

A LIST OF POPULAR EQUESTRIAN ORGANIZATIONS

FOR RIDERS 18 AND UNDER

Athletic Equestrian League (AEL) www.athleticequestrian.com: English and Western riders in grades 1-12 can participate in competitions that include flat classes, jumping or patterns, and a horsemanship knowledge phase.

Interscholastic Equestrian Association (IEA) www.rideiea.org: Provides competitive and educational opportunities in hunt seat, western, and dressage for riders in grades 4-12.

Intercollegiate Horse Shows Association (IHSA) www.ihsainc.com: North American organization for college-level competition in English and Western equitation.

US Pony Club (USPC) www.ponyclub.org: Riding clubs in the US and Canada that teach about riding, horse care, and barn management. In Great Britain, known as the Pony Club.

4-H https://4-h.org: Local organizations that focus on certain activities, such as horses.

BREEDS

Although a few breed-specific groups are mentioned here, virtually all breeds, including color breeds, have sites you can visit.

American Morgan Horse Association www.morganhorse.com: (AMHA) Promoting the Morgan breed, AMHA has affiliations with Morgan breed Assocs world-wide.

American Quarter Horse Association (AQHA) www.aqha.com: The largest breed organization in the world.

The Jockey Club www.jockeyclub.com: The US and Canadian registry for Thoroughbreds.

COMPETITIONS

International Equestrian Federation (FEI) www.fei.org: Worldwide governing body for equestrian sports of showjumping, para-equestrian, driving, dressage, eventing, endurance, and vaulting.

US Equestrian Federation (USEF) www.usef.org: Governing body for all horse sports in the US including the US Eventing Assoc (USEA), US Hunter/Jumper Assoc (USHJA), and the US Dressage Assoc (USDF).

SPORTS

American Driving Society (ADS) www.americandrivingsociety.com: Excellent resource for driving in US and Canada.

International Professional Rodeo Association (IPRA) www.iprarodeo.com: The governing body for rodeo, with competitors from all over the world.

Master of Fox Hounds Association (MFHA) https://mfha.com: In the US, Canada, and Great Britain, this is the place for all things foxhunting.

North American Trail Ride Conference (NATRC) https://natrc.org: Information on how to get started and participate in long distance trail riding competitions.

US Polo Association (USPA) www.uspolo.org: The place to go if you want to watch and where to learn how to play.

RESOURCES

Although these are professional organizations, they offer a lot of good information and are excellent resources for finding the professional help you want.

American Association of Equine Practitioners (AAEP) www.aaep.org: Equine health management.

American Riding Instructors Association (ARIA) www.aria.org: Certification for instructors in many disciplines and horse care.

Certified Horsemanship Association (CHA) https://cha.horse: Certification and continuing education programs for professional instructors.

GLOSSARY

Baler: A piece of farm equipment pulled by a tractor that scoops up cut hay and compresses it into bales, generally rectangles, that weigh about 40 lbs. Each bale is made of smaller sections, called flakes, by which the bale is easily divided into portions.

Balk: A reluctance to move forward, or an attempt to back away, generally from something that is perceived to be a threat, or a situation a horse wants to avoid.

Bars (of the hoof): The rigid, raised area on the outer edges of the clefts, or sulci, next to the frog.

Bars (of the mouth): The space on both the upper and lower jaws that separates the incisors, or front teeth, from the molars to the rear. This is where the bit sits in a horse's mouth.

Bars (on the saddle): The metal bar from which the stirrup leather hangs, located under the skirt of the saddle.

Check Ligament: A special ligament at the stifle joint of a horse that they can use to stabilize one hind leg, allowing the opposite leg to rest.

Chestnut: Besides a color, chestnuts are rough scaly patches found on the inside of a horse's legs. They can grow quite large, but are dead tissue, so can be easily trimmed. They are what remains of the hoof covering from prehistoric horses.

Colic: A general term used for a stomach ache in a horse. It can be mild to severe.

Concentrates: A term for feeds produced from a variety of ingredients, then steam and compressed into pellets. Not the same as whole grains, such as oats or corn, but may contain both.

Dapples: Faint, circular areas of lighter hair in the coat, usually found on the rump, hindquarters, or belly, but can be anywhere. Often an indication of a healthy coat.

GLOSSARY

Flaxen: A lighter color of the mane and tail, ranging from a cream color to almost white.

Flea-bitten: On gray horses, the appearance of small, darker flecks of hair, generally found all over the body, but particularly the neck area.

Girth: The piece of tack that runs under the horse's belly from one side of the saddle to the other in order to keep it firmly on the horse's back. Also, the area of the body that it covers.

Grullo: A type of dun coloring, generally a darkish gray. Grullos have a dorsal stripe, and often a dark or black mask on the face and zebra stripes on the upper portion of the legs.

Hands: The unit of measure indicating the height of a horse from the ground near the front hoof straight up to the top of the wither at the base of the neck. One hand equals four inches.

Heartgirth: The circumference of the horse's body when measured just behind the front legs. The girth of the saddle runs along the same line.

Internal Parasites: Also known as worms, these larvae include pinworms, bots, tapeworms, strongyles, and ascarids. They can cause numerous issues including weight loss, poor condition, colic, and intestinal damage.

Intravenous: Indicates something being introduced directly into a vein, as in medications or fluids.

Muzzle: The soft area between the nostrils of the horse, and above the upper lip.

pH level: pH refers to the level of acidity of a material. For the digestive system to function well, its normal pH range must be kept in check.

Points: When referring to coat colors, the points are the muzzle and lips, the edge of the ears, the lower legs, the mane, and the tail.

Post mortem: An internal examination performed after death to help determine the cause.

Przewalski's horse: Brought back from the brink of extinction by breeding in captivity, Equus ferus przewalskii is the only true wild horse alive today.

GLOSSARY | 193

Quick-tie: Or quick release knot. A safe way to tie a horse to a fixed object. The knot is made to slip apart relatively easily by pulling on the tail end. This allows a person to free the horse if there is trouble without getting too close to a possibly panicking animal.

Rabies: An infectious viral disease of mammals that causes neurological symptoms such as madness and convulsions, and eventually death. Transmitted by bites from infected animals through saliva.

Rain rot: A fungal infection of the skin in which small scabs form that eventually slough off removing the hair and leaving the skin tender. Most commonly found along the back and around the pasterns when horses are left ungroomed or standing in wet conditions for prolonged periods. Prevention is the best cure.

Roughage: Any type of high fiber feed for a horse. Forage like grass and hay are roughage. Beet pulp is a good dietary addition if horses need supplemental fiber.

Shy: A movement away from an area or object that is either unfamiliar or perceived as dangerous.

Sorrel: A coat color like a chestnut but with a distinctly lighter mane and tail.

Splint: Small bones (formerly part of a prehistoric horse's toes) on the inside of a horse's cannon bones, splints can fracture or pull away from the bones, causing usually temporary lameness until the area repairs.

Spook: A quick action to the back, side, or front when the horse is startled or frightened; a sudden move to get away from something.

Tack: The general term for the equipment used to ride a horse, including the saddle, girth, saddle pad, stirrups, bridle, reins, and bit.

Tetanus: An incurable, but rare, non-transmissible bacterial infection. Found in soil and manure, tetanus is often contracted through a wound like a puncture. Tetanus causes severe muscle spasms and can inhibit breathing, leading to death.

Thrush: A fungal infection of the hoof. Thrush is naturally occurring in most types of soil. It becomes an infection when it is allowed to take hold and flourish in a hoof, particularly around the frog and clefts. Although easy to treat, if left unattended it can cause serious damage to the frog and heel area. Easily prevented by picking feet daily and ensuring the horse has a clean, dry area.

Torsion: A twist of one of the areas of a horse's intestinal tract that prevents the normal flow of matter through the system. Rarely treatable without surgery.

Weaning: The process of a foal transferring from the mare's milk to grass, hay, and grain for food. Horses in the wild will wean their young by the time they are yearlings. Typically done by humans around six months of age by separating the pair for longer and longer periods while offering the foal different foods.

Withers: The prominence of the spinal processes above the shoulder. They indicate where the neck ends and the back begins. Typically the highest point of the back, and used for measuring the height of the horse; saddles sit just behind the withers.

ABOUT THE AUTHOR

Elisa King is the author of *The Complete Guide to Your First Horse for Young Riders* and *Physiology to Become a Better Horseman and Have a Deeper Bond With Your Partner*.

Her work is focused on animals, delving into the fascinating world of horses, pets, and farm animals, and providing guidance on animal care.

Elisa has spent her life in the company of animals. She developed a particular interest in horses, and with a passion for learning, she threw herself into equine studies. Her goal now is to share her knowledge and lead more people to reap the benefits of knowing more about these magnificent creatures.

REFERENCES

American Museum of Natural History. (2019). *The evolution of horses.* American Museum of Natural History. https://www.amnh.org/exhibitions/horse/the-evolution-of-horses

AZQuotes. (n.d.). *A quote from Benjamin Disreali.* Www.azquotes.com. Retrieved March 25, 2023, from https://www.azquotes.com/citation/quote/398894

B, A. (2022, May 29). *Mane Braiding FAQ: Hunter vs. Dressage Braids.* Horse Rookie. https://horserookie.com/hunter-dressage-braiding-manes/

Beyer, G. (2022, November 2). *5 famous horses and their roles in history.* TheCollector. https://www.thecollector.com/5-famous-horses-throughout-history/

Blocksdorf, K. (2019a, June 1). *Discover the differences between a horse and a pony.* The Spruce Pets. https://www.thesprucepets.com/the-difference-between-horses-and-ponies-1886998

Blocksdorf, K. (2019b, September 15). *Here's how to identify your horse's leg markings.* The Spruce Pets. https://www.thesprucepets.com/leg-markings-on-horses-1887398

Blocksdorf, K. (2019c, September 16). *Recognize horse facial markings such as blazes, stars and snips.* The Spruce Pets. https://www.thesprucepets.com/horse-facial-markings-1887393

Bowen, E. L. (2000). *Man o' War.* Eclipse Press.

BrainyQuotes. (n.d.). *Benjamin Franklin quotes.* BrainyQuote. Retrieved March 25, 2023, from https://www.brainyquote.com/quotes/benjamin_franklin_151591

Buckley, D. (2019, December 17). *All about the cremello horse.* I Heart Horses. https://ihearthorses.com/all-about-the-beautiful-cremello-horse/

Copper Mare Media, Ltd. (2013). *Horse colors in pictures.* Equine Spot. https://www.equinespot.com/horse-colors.html

198 | REFERENCES

Cowboy Magic. (2014, June 2). *20 Horse Quotes.* Cowboy Magic. https://cowboymagic.com/20-horse-quotes-cowboy-magic/

Downs, J. F. (1961). *The origin and spread of riding in the near East and Central Asia.* American Anthropologist, 63(6), 1193–1203. https://doi.org/10.1525/aa.1961.63.6.02a00030

EquiWorld.net. (n.d.). *Horses - how do horses chew? Equine dentistry.* Retrieved March 15, 2023, from http://www.equiworld.net/horses/horsecare/dentist/straightfromthehorsesmouth/howdohorseschew.htm

Fairchild, C. (2021). *Our connection to horses* [Clinic Presentation].

Fowler, J. (2020). *30 feel good horse riding quotes!* Paddock Blade Australia. https://paddockblade.com.au/blogs/paddock-blade-blog/30-horse-riding-quotes

G, M. (2022, September 9). *How strong is a horse kick? (& can it kill you?!).* Equestrian Boots and Bridles. https://equestrianbootsandbridles.com/how-strong-is-a-horse-kick-can-it-kill-you/

Gessner, C., & Smith, C. (2017, November 3). *Phylogeny of equids.* Wikimedia. https://commons.wikimedia.org/wiki/File:Equus_phylogeny_%28eng%29.png

Goodreads. (n.d.-a). *A quote by Walter Farley.* Www.goodreads.com. Retrieved March 20, 2023, from https://www.goodreads.com/quotes/3227988-yet-when-books-have-been-read-and-reread-it-boils

Goodreads. (n.d.-b). *A quote by Winston S. Churchill.* Www.goodreads.com. Retrieved March 22, 2023, from https://www.goodreads.com/quotes/22166-there-is-something-about-the-outside-of-a-horse-that

Goosewing Ranch. (2012, September 15). *Horse speed.* Goosewing Ranch. https://goosewingranch.com/tag/horse-speed/

Grant, Y. (2016). *The little red book of horse wisdom.* Skyhorse Publishing.

Handwerk, B. (2021, February 2). *An evolutionary timeline of homo sapiens.* Smithsonian Magazine. https://www.smithsonianmag.com%2Fscience-nature%2Fessential-timeline-understanding-evolution-homo-sapiens-180976807

Henneke, et al. (1983). *Equine body condition scoring.* https://vetmed.

tamu.edu/files/vetmed/vmth/laminitis/ Equine_Body_Condition_Scoring.pdf

Henry, Miles. (2020, November 30). *Dun vs. buckskin horses, what's the difference? 5 clues.* Horse Racing Sense. https://horseracingsense.com/dun-vs-buckskin-horses-whats-the-difference/

Herbermann, E. F. (2003). *A horseman's notes.* J.A. Allen.

Hertz, K. (2022, February 9). *Mystery of Shergar, the champion horse who was kidnapped in Ireland.* Irish Central. https://www.irishcentral.com/roots/history/shergar-irish-horse-kidnap

History Editors. (2018, August 21). *Secretariat.* History. https://www.history.com/topics/sports/secretariat

Horseque. (2022, October 22). *200+ horse quotes and saying that will make you smile.* Inspirational. https://horseque.com/inspirational-funny-love-and-cute-horse-quotes

Issel, DVM, C. (2002, June 18). *Coggins test.* American Association of Equine Practitioners. https://aaep.org/issue/coggins-test

Lee, A. (2019, September 3). *Paint horse vs. pinto vs. skewbald vs. piebald.* Helpful Horse Hints. https://www.helpfulhorsehints.com/paint-horse-vs-pinto-vs-skewbald-vs-piebald/

Lee, A. (2020, April 7). *11 ways you can measure horse weight + average weights by breed & height.* Helpful Horse Hints. https://www.helpfulhorsehints.com/measuring-horse-weight/

Letts, E. (2011). *The Eighty-Dollar Champion.* Ballantine Books.

Lewis, C. S. (1976). *The horse and his boy.* Macmillan.

Liburt, N., Malinowski, K., & Williams, C. (2016, November). *Measuring temperature, pulse, & respiration (TPR): What's normal for my horse?* Rutgers University. https://esc.rutgers.edu/fact_sheet/measuring-tpr/

Ludovic, O. (2021, October 20). *Origin of domestic horses finally established.* Centre Nationale de la Recherche Scientifique. https://www.cnrs.fr/en/origin-domestic-horses-finally-established

Martin, C. (2017, September 14). *Choose the right forage mix for your grazing needs.* Farm and Dairy. https://www.farmanddairy.com/columns/choose-the-right-forge-mix-for-your-grazing-needs/443255.html

Maugh II, Thomas. (1988, February 16). *New light shed on cavemen and killing of horses*. Los Angeles Times. https://www.latimes.com/archives/la-xpm-1988-02-16-mn-42976-story.html

Mauldin, L. (2018, September 20). *Jumping in jockey stirrups: Steeplechase 101*. The Plaid Horse Magazine. https://www.theplaidhorse.com/2018/09/20/jumping-in-jockey-stirrups-steeplechase-101/

Oke, DVM, S. (2018, July 16). *Journey through the equine GI tract*. The Horse. https://thehorse.com/159348/journey-through-the-equine-gi-tract/

Oser, C. (2017, June 16). *Secretariat's heart size: Inside the tremendous machine*. Horse Racing Nation. https://www.horseracingnation.com/news/The_Tremendous_Size_of_Secretariat_s_Heart_123

Ours, D. (2013). *Battleship: A daring heiress, a teenage jockey, and America's horse*. St. Martin's Press.

Randall, Keith. (2015, March 23). *Ice-Age hunters were in North America earlier than believed*. Texas A&M Today. https://today.tamu.edu/2015/03/23/ice-age-hunters-were-in-north-america-earlier-than-believed/

Rashid, M. (2019). *A good horse is never a bad color*. Simon and Schuster.

Robinson, L. (2023). *How hard can a horse kick?* Horse Factbook. https://www.horsefactbook.com/trivia/how-hard-do-horses-kick/

Rouge, M. (2019). *Aging horses by their teeth*. Colorado State University. http://www.vivo.colostate.edu/hbooks/pathphys/digestion/pregastric/aginghorses.html

Selby, K. (2019). *Balance three ways*. Riding Instructor Magazine, Winter 2018-2019.

Show Jumping Hall of Fame. (2021, September 9). *The legend of Harry deLeyer's Snowman*. Horse Network. https://horsenetwork.com/2021/09/halloffamethursday-the-legend-of-harry-deleyers-snowman/

Smith, S. (2019, September 28). *8 oldest horses in history that lived to be very old*. Horsey Hooves. https://horseyhooves.com/oldest-horses-in-history/

Smithsonian National Zoo. (2018, December 19). *Przewalski's horse*.

REFERENCES | 201

National Zoo Smithsonian. https://nationalzoo.si.edu/animals/przewalskis-horse

Stange, E. (2022, October 3). *Video: Opinion / pony boys.* The New York Times. https://www.nytimes.com/video/opinion/100000008461716/pony-boys.html?smid=nytcore-ios-share&referringSource=articleShare

The Equinest. (2013). *Black base horse coat color.* The Equinest.http://www.theequinest.com/colors/base/black/

Trvst. (2022, October 24). *30 horse quotes to inspire freedom and companionship.* TRVST. https://www.trvst.world/biodiversity/horse-quotes/

US National Park Service. (2021, October 12). *Prehistoric life of Tule Springs ancient horse.* National Park Service. https://www.nps.gov/articles/000/ancient-horse.htm

Waite, K. (2015, August 30). *Impaction colic in horses.* MSU Extension. https://www.canr.msu.edu/news/impaction_colic_in_horses

Williams, S. C. P. (2012, May 7). *Whence the domestic horse?* Science. https://www.science.org/content/article/whence-domestic-horse

Wood, C. (2020, January 22). *Temperature, pulse and respiration in a horse.* Horses Extension. https://horses.extension.org/temperature-pulse-and-respiration-in-a-horse/

IMAGE REFERENCES

Alexa. (2017). *Horse brushing* [Image]. Pixabay. https://pixabay.com/photos/horse-love-horse-clean-brush-curry-2818959

Alexa. (2017). *Open box in-and-out* [Image]. Pixabay. https://pixabay.com/photos/horse-brown-barn-box-cute-2776880

Anthony, J. (2007). *TB jockeys racing* [Image]. Pexels. https://www.pexels.com/photo/jockeys-riding-their-horses-11341149/

Bair, C. (2020). *Dandy brush* [Image]. Unsplash. https://unsplash.com/photos/sJBBCn4vk8Y

Boys In Bristol Photography. (2022). *Black horse with star* [Image].

Pexels. https://www.pexels.com/photo/close-up-of-a-black-horse-13809853/

Claire, R. (2018). *Horse in bridle* [Image]. Pexels. https://www.pexels.com/photo/muzzle-of-horse-in-stall-4846365/

Dandelion Tea. (2020). *Coat colors* [Image]. Pixabay. https://pixabay.com/vectors/horse-horses-coat-color-5477507/

Dids. (2019). *Gray horse snip* [Image]. Pexels. https://www.pexels.com/photo/person-holding-white-horse-2332834/

Dulude, D. (2021). *Almost angry* [Image]. Pexels. https://www.pexels.com/photo/a-horse-on-a-farm-10259372/

Dunlop, I. (2015). *Pony jumping* [Image]. Pixabay. https://pixabay.com/photos/white-horse-jumping-child-white-965618/

Johnson, L. (2016). *Western tack* [Image]. Pixabay. https://pixabay.com/photos/cowboy-horse-dog-pasture-western-1130695

Kammermann, K. (2022). *Farrier* [Image]. Pixabay. https://pixabay.com/photos/farrier-hoof-care-horse-7118941/

Klinsmann, L. (2017). *Hunter show rider no stirrups* [Image]. Pexels. https://www.pexels.com/photo/depth-of-field-photography-of-woman-riding-brown-horse-883630/

Krijgsman, A. (2016). *English tack* [Image]. Pexels. https://www.pexels.com/photo/brown-horse-with-black-saddle-4019299

Laugesen, J. (2017). *Black colt* [Image]. Pexels. https://www.pexels.com/photo/black-horse-running-on-grass-field-with-flowers-634613/

Envato Elements, DegrooteStock, Saddle against shabby wooden stable. https://elements.envato.com/saddle-against-shabby-wooden-stable-ZBG8MNJ

Envato Elements, tristana, Black English saddle hanging on fence near stables. https://elements.envato.com/black-english-saddle-hanging-on-fence-near-stables-PT5Z4C2

Envato Elements, PixelSquid360, Horse 3d. https://elements.envato.com/fr/horse-HF5CER

Kobayashi, M. (2019). Horse hoof cleaning [Image]. In Pixabay. https://pixabay.com/photos/horse-animal-zoo-hoof-cleaning-4598785/

Menke, J. (2014). *Chestnut foal blaze* [Image]. Pexels. https://www.pexels.com/photo/brown-horse-on-green-grass-field-5732891/

REFERENCES | 203

Morissy, B. (2020). *Double run-in shed* [Image]. Unsplash. https://unsplash.com/photos/tpADyvS9AAU
NoName_13. (2018). *Trail ride* [Image]. Pixabay. https://pixabay.com/photos/ride-out-horse-riding-equestrian-3788373
Olsen, B. (2021a). *Haybales* [Image]. Pexels. https://www.pexels.com/photo/photo-of-a-woman-in-a-green-jacket-carrying-hay-7882607
Olsen, B. (2021b). *Picking a hoof* [Image]. Pexels. https://www.pexels.com/photo/a-person-cleaning-a-horse-s-hoof-7882339/
Plenio, J. (2018). *Leopard appaloosa* [Image]. Pexels. https://www.pexels.com/photo/horse-eating-grass-1574546/
Russo, G. H. (2018). *Dun and paint* [Image]. Pixabay. https://pixabay.com/horses-classmates-equines-animals-3465412/
S., K. (2017). *Colorful horse pinto* [Image]. Pixabay. https://pixabay.com/photos/colorful-horse-traffic-run-pasture-2388277/
Smid, E. (2015). *Horse skull teeth* [Image]. Pixabay. https://pixabay.com/photos/skull-death-horse-teeth-anatomy-646628/
Stockli, S. (2019). *Icelandic ponies* [Image]. Pixabay. https://pixabay.com/photos/animals-icelandic-horses-mammal-4649468
TheOtherKev. (2019). *Tidy barn aisle* [Image]. Pixabay. https://pixabay.com/photos/stable-girl-horses-animals-barn-4426781
Thornebrooke, A. (2022). *Gray in stall* [Image]. Unsplash. https://unsplash.com/photos/SvChZO-y7GI
van Hartesvelt, M. (2015). *Bald face* [Image]. Pixabay. https://pixabay.com/photos/horse-farm-field-equine-equestrian-920435/
Wetzler, S. (2016). *Horse muzzle teeth* [Image]. Pixabay. https://pixabay.com/photos/horse-horse-muzzle-gluttonous-mould-1766790/

Printed in Poland
by Amazon Fulfillment
Poland Sp. z o.o., Wrocław
31 August 2023